The Unusual Suspects

The Unusual Suspects

25 Jewish people defy the final taboo

Richard Gibson

CHRISTIAN
FOCUS

IBSN 978 1 84550 414 4

Copyright © Richard Gibson 2008

Published in 2008 by
Christian Focus Publications, Geanies House,
Fearn, Ross-shire, IV20 1TW, Scotland.

www.christianfocus.com

Cover design by Daniel Van Straaten

Printed and bound by Norhaven A/S, Denmark.

Contents

Introduction 7

The Most Special Relationship of All – *Julian* 15

Paying the Price – *Bernard* 21

There and Back Again – *Anita* 29

From Pain to Peace – *Esme* 35

From Russia With Love! – *Sonya* 41

Desperately Seeking Truth – *Gil* 45

Somebody Knocking On My Door – *Lynda* 55

From Hamburg by Kindertransport – *Ruth* 63

They Drink Blood! – *Rita* 71

All about Eve – *Eve* 77

Light from the Tanakh – *Tony* 83

An Everlasting Love – *Joseph* 89

Hear, O Israel – *Debbie* 95

Headhunters and Revolution – *James* 101

The Most Important Day of my Life – *Marie* 107

It's a Wonderful Life – *Sheila* 111

God in an Unexpected Place – *Rosamund* 115

Twice Chosen – *Peter* 121

The Glass is Full! – *Estelle* 127

That Unspeakable Name – *Barry*.. 135

My Sweet Lord – *Deborah* 141

Journey of Discovery – *Yacov*.. 155

From New Age to New Life – *Sarah*... 163

Not Ashamed – *Joe* 167

Shalom at the Jesus Tent! – *Gerry* 175

Glossary 181

Introduction

"Messianic Jews" are an enigma to both the Jewish community and the Christian Church. For many Jewish people, the idea that one can be both Jewish and a believer in Jesus is as logical as the notion of a kosher pig. One rabbi characterises Jews who believe in Jesus as vulnerable, lonely, elderly, poor, emotionally unstable, and naive. "These unfortunates", he states, "are lured into accepting [Christian] doctrines out of emotional need, not intellectual conviction."

Very few Christians know much about the Jewish people and, sadly, far too many are influenced by traditional attitudes that stereotype Jews as killers of the Messiah and therefore the implacable enemies of Christianity. As a result, Jews who believe in Jesus are seen as an anomaly because, after all, "Jews don't believe in Jesus". Indeed, some Church dignitaries teach that Jewish people *should* not believe in Jesus.

Many people suspect that Jesus is for Gentiles and that the world would be a better place if the nations took the Sermon on the Mount seriously. But *Jewish* believers in Jesus! They are the unusual suspects. Who would suspect that it is likely that more Jewish people believe in Jesus today than at any time in history? Even the rabbi quoted above claims that more Jews have become Christians in the last 20 years than in the last 2,000.

However, the reality is people don't become Messianic Jews to have an easier life: for everyone misunderstands them! So why do they do it? The answer to that question is what this book is all about.

The Unusual Suspects

As far as some people are concerned, then, the book you have in your hand is about a group of people who should not exist. But they do exist and here are their stories. Some are young, some are old, others are somewhere in between; some are from religious backgrounds while, for others, God was once not so important. The accounts are fresh, honest, gritty and unusual but all the stories have one thing in common, they are about Jewish people who have come to believe that Yeshua is the Messiah of Israel and the Saviour of the world. Each of them has encountered a vibrant truth that compelled them to take a step that has put them out of step with the majority of their people. Their honesty will, of course, leave them open to the criticism that they were vulnerable and weak and needed a crutch. But that claim begs two big questions. First of all, what's wrong with a crutch if you're crippled? Secondly, if what you believe in can't support you when you are "vulnerable and weak" why not find something that does?

Many Jewish religious leaders are uncomfortable with people who not only believe in Yeshua but also continue to identify themselves as Jews. The emotive rhetoric directed towards these Messianic Jews, especially in Israel in the towns of Arad and Beer Sheva, has at times spilled over into intimidation and violence. One British Messianic Jew recalls that when he was planning to immigrate to Israel his aliyah agent called to ask if he believed Yeshua was the Mashiach. Even as he answered yes, he said in his heart, "Goodbye my beautiful homeland; hello ever-deepening exile."

But not all Jewish leaders feel intimidated by Jews who follow Yeshua. Reform Rabbi Dan Cohn-Sherbok has challenged what he calls "the final taboo of Jewishness". In his book *Messianic Judaism* Rabbi Cohn-Sherbok calls for the reintegration of Messianic Jews into the Jewish community, while Reconstructionist Rabbi Carol Harris-Shapiro asserts that Messianic Judaism is simultaneously a form of Judaism and a form of Christianity. Her most prominent book on the subject is *Messianic Judaism: a Rabbi's Journey through Religious Change in America.*

So there are Jews who believe in Jesus and their existence is acknowledged by some prominent Jewish leaders. But how is it possible to be both Jewish and Christian? Our unusual suspects might not be Messianic *Jews* at all. Might they not just be Christians who *used* to be Jewish?

Who's who?
It might help if we define our terms. First of all, who is a Jew? The most basic biblical definition is that a Jew is someone who is descended from Abraham, Isaac and

Jacob and, if a male, has been circumcised. Many Jewish friends have told me on numerous occasions, "I was born a Jew and I will die a Jew."

So if we can define Jewishness in its basic form in terms of biology (even though many Orthodox Jews see it as more than that), what is a Christian? The term "Christian" was coined in the Syrian city of Antioch in the first century CE as an uncomplimentary nickname for the huge numbers of Greek-speaking Jews who believed in the *Christos*, the Greek word for Messiah[1]. The first followers of Yeshua called themselves followers of *haDerekh*, "The Way", a title Yeshua used to describe himself[2]. In one of his speeches recorded in the New Testament, the apostle Paul admits to persecuting "the followers of this Way" while he had been a young man [3].

One of the great forgotten facts of history is that the first followers of "The Way" were all Jewish! The first council of the Church was held not in Rome but in Jerusalem. The New Testament book *The Acts of the Apostles* records that the leaders of the Church convened the Jerusalem council to discuss whether it was possible for someone to be a genuine Christian if they were not Jewish![4] How times have changed! It sounds bizarre when we consider that the big issue today is: "Can someone be a follower of Jesus if they *are* Jewish?"

It is a serious mistake to imagine that people are Christian because they were born in a "Christian" country or into a "Christian" family. In every nation and culture there are people who claim to have "met" the Bethlehem-born Jewish rabbi called Yeshua, and believe he is the one promised by the ancient Hebrew prophets. They believe he is the divine Messiah who died for the sins of the world and was raised from the dead three days after his death, as foretold in the Jewish Scriptures![5]

The Jewish people in this book have each made a journey of discovery that has connected them with God through Yeshua the Messiah. Have they "converted"? That depends what is meant by "converted". Conversion, "turning back", *t'shuva* is a perfectly good Jewish concept. But if we use "conversion" in the sense of turning *away*, there is no such thing as a "converted Jew" because Jewishness is not a sin. In the sense of "turning away", there are only converted sinners. The stories in this book, therefore, are of Jewish people who performed the ultimate *shuva*; they turned from sin, turned to their Messiah and turned back to the God of Abraham, Isaac and Jacob.

What about "the Church"? The term conjures up images of vast gothic structures and elaborate rituals but when Yeshua told his first disciples that he would build his *ekklesia*, his "church", none of them asked him what a "church" was. Jewish people in the Diaspora were familiar with the concept of Israel being God's *ekklesia* – the Greek equivalent of the Hebrew *kahal* – his assembly, his congregation, his... *church*! In the first century CE many Jewish people were dissatisfied with Israel's religious leadership, and groups like the Essenes branched off and formed their own assemblies which, according to them, reflected the true essence of what it was to be Jewish. All those groups died out but Yeshua continued to build his assembly, which today is a worldwide phenomenon.

Why not?
So, here are the stories of people who follow Yeshua but continue to identify themselves as Jews. And why not?

According to the New Testament, Christianity is Jewish. The very word "Christian" derives from *Christos*, the Greek equivalent of *Mashiach* or "Anointed One".

Some Jewish thinkers have suggested that Yeshua may be "Christ" for the Christians but he is not the Messiah for the Jewish people. However, if Yeshua is not the Messiah for Israel, how can he be the Saviour of the world?

I am indebted to each of the people whose story appears in this book. As I interviewed some, and read and edited the stories of others I was deeply moved by the honesty and the power of their narratives. This book is not about the famous or the perfect. *The Unusual Suspects* is about normal lives made extraordinary by divine love.

As you read these stories, you may disagree with the faith choice these people have made, Messianic Jews are a misunderstood and misrepresented group, but at least you can now understand for yourself some of the reasons why they believe in Yeshua. Others may say, "Why can't I have the experience these people have had?" Well, you can, it's up to you! The implications of accepting the invitation of Yeshua to follow him are great. As history's most famous Messianic Jew said concerning his own experience:

> ... circumcised on the eighth day, of the people of Israel, of the tribe of Benjamin, a Hebrew of Hebrews; as to the law, a Pharisee; as to zeal, a persecutor of the church; as to righteousness under the law, blameless. But whatever gain I had, I counted as loss for the sake of the Messiah. Indeed, I count everything as loss because of the surpassing worth of knowing Messiah Yeshua my

Lord. For his sake I have suffered the loss of all things and count them as rubbish, in order that I may gain Messiah and be found in him, not having a righteousness of my own that comes from the law, but that which comes through faith in Messiah.[6]

Endnotes

[1] Acts of the Apostles 11:26. "Barnabas went to Tarsus to look for Saul, and when he had found him, he brought him to Antioch. For a whole year they met with the church and taught a great many people. And in Antioch the disciples were first called Christians."

[2] Gospel of John 14:6. "Thomas said to him, 'Lord, we do not know where you are going. How can we know the way?' Jesus said to him, 'I am the way, and the truth, and the life. No one comes to the Father except through me'."

[3] Acts of the Apostles 22:4. "And when they heard that he was addressing them in the Hebrew language, they became even more quiet. And he said: 'I am a Jew, born in Tarsus in Cilicia, but brought up in this city, educated at the feet of Gamaliel according to the strict manner of the law of our fathers, being zealous for God as all of you are this day. I persecuted this Way to the death, binding and delivering to prison both men and women'."

[4] Acts of the Apostles 15:1,2. "Some men came down from Judea and were teaching the brothers, 'Unless you are circumcised according to the custom of Moses, you cannot be saved.' And after Paul and Barnabas had no small dissension and debate with them, Paul and Barnabas and some of the others were appointed to go up to Jerusalem to the apostles and the elders about this question."

[5] First Letter to the Corinthians 15:4. "I delivered to you as of first importance what I also received: that the Messiah died for our sins in accordance with the Tanakh, that he was buried, that he was raised on the third day in accordance with the Tanakh."

[6] Letter to the Philippians 3:5-9.

The Most Special Relationship of All

Julian

I was born and raised in a quite traditional Orthodox Jewish family that was originally from India. We were a large, extended, close and warm-hearted family. I attended synagogue with my father most Saturdays and on all of the main Jewish festivals.

I grew up with a fear of and reverence for God but, in hindsight, I didn't know the love of God. As for Yeshua, he was never really mentioned or, when he was, it was normally in the context of, "Oh! He was a great prophet". So, in practice, Yeshua was just comfortably categorised, put aside and not really dealt with. After my Bar Mitzvah, my synagogue attendance ceased because I was able to convince my father that playing football for my school was a much better way of spending my time on Shabbat. Football was the love of my life (my wife would probably tell you that it still is!) so, from the age of fourteen, it took only a few years for me to first of all marginalize God and then ignore him altogether. From then on, I really did whatever I wanted to do; which meant I did pretty much everything.

Was it fun? I thought it was fun for a while, but ultimately it wasn't. I found myself leading a quite empty and aimless life for many years.

Nobody's Fool

I won't regale you with all the twists, turns and coincidences that led me to meet and start going out with my wife Alison, but back in 1993, she was my girlfriend. I knew she was a committed Christian and, in my arrogance, I found her faith faintly amusing at first, but later I found it very threatening. Alison was always trying to persuade me to go to church with her, as she hoped that I would join her in her belief in Yeshua as the Messiah. At that time she attended the 11am Sunday service at All Souls in Langham Place, London, and she wanted me to attend a *Christianity Explained* course held there on Monday nights.

"Fat chance!" I thought to myself. "Here I am; I'm an intelligent man, I'm a lawyer, I'm a sceptic. I know my stuff; I'm nobody's fool. Not for me!"

"Apart from anything else," I thought, "I am a Jew". The Christian world has traditionally been a hostile place for Jews, and I wasn't about to go willingly to a place I believed was full of my enemies. But my most immediate and tangible excuse for getting out of church and the *Christianity Explained* course was, "Look, I play five a-side football at 11am on Sundays and 7pm on Mondays!" Wow, what a coincidence. Couldn't do it – sorry.

I played in a team where if you lost your place, even for a week, you would be out of the squad for many weeks, maybe months. "I'm not having it," I told Alison, adding, "And that is that!" Except it wasn't, because what I didn't know then but do know now, is that we can't fight God's will, much as we might try.

The Mystery Footballer

Within a few months, another player turned up on Sundays. He wasn't anyone that we knew, and no one knew where he had come from. Everyone assumed he was a friend of a friend and that he was filling in. Anyway, one day he fouled me really badly. I don't think he meant to do it, but it was terrible and my football career was brought to an abrupt and shattering end. With my football went my most tangible excuse for not going to church with Alison. To placate her, I did go along to *Christianity Explained* at All Souls but it's fair to say that I took with me not only considerable reservations, which in my eyes were insurmountable, but also considerable hostility.

Bombshell

So I did the course. I found that, even approaching it from the standpoint of a highly sceptical lawyer, I couldn't actually pick holes in what I was being taught and shown. And that was a real surprise to me, I can tell you. What was more of a surprise was that I agreed to do the six-week course all over again.

I was interested in finding out more about Jesus, but it was also very unsettling for me and, to be frank, I don't know why I agreed to do it again. But I did.

It was about that time that Alison dropped a bombshell.

She had been going through inner torment which, I guess, I already knew. She said that it was the only time in her life that she had felt God was speaking to her. She believed that she must end our relationship. That was a very tough time for us. It was heartbreaking, because I wanted to be with Alison and she wanted to be with me. But I couldn't pretend to be something that I wasn't. Furthermore, I still viewed the prospect of believing in Yeshua in terms of switching cultural identities and thought that becoming a follower of Yeshua would be a betrayal of my Jewish heritage. It was an unimaginable prospect for me, and I just couldn't see it happening.

We were fortunate to receive wise and supportive counselling from the leader of the *Christianity Explained* group. He himself was from an Indian background, so I think he understood quite well what I was going through. To cut a long story short, I decided to see the course through, but in my heart I didn't expect anything to come of it. Also, I had begun to come to terms with the prospect of ending my relationship with Alison. What I never, never expected was that I was close to the start of the most special relationship of all.

Wake Up and Smell the Coffee
One Sunday morning, while Alison was attending the service at All Souls, I was waiting for her in a café round the corner from Langham Place. I had my breakfast and a coffee in front of me, three heavy Sunday newspapers to read which, for me, was just fine. But I also had a Bible with me to do my *Christianity Explained* homework from the Gospel of Mark. I thought that it would take only a few minutes, so I decided to get it out of the way first.

The next thing I knew, an hour and a half had passed. My coffee was cold and the breakfast uneaten. The newspapers were unopened, for I had realised that I was reading the truth, pure and simple. I had found the Gospel of Mark exhilarating. I suddenly knew that Yeshua was alive and was my Messiah. I think I discovered what the first followers of Yeshua must have felt. For me it was as though Yeshua had recently been crucified and had risen from the dead, and I had just heard the good news of his resurrection. I felt such a tremendous sense of excitement. I had never known it before, but I quickly came to see that, as a Jewish person, I had come into my full inheritance.

However, my sense of elation was quickly followed by a feeling of panic as I began to realise the consequences that following Yeshua would have on my life. What of my identity? What of my Jewish heritage? Most of all, what of my family and my Jewish friends? What a mountain I had to climb in terms of my family and friends! I know I could never have seen it through alone, but I did not have to because God held my hand every step of the way. Obstacles – and there were many of them – were miraculously removed, even as they arose!

Alison and I were married in December 1996. It was a miracle that every single member of my large, extended Jewish family, and all of my friends, came to the ceremony. Some even commented on how moving they found it, even though Yeshua was so central to the ceremony.

Our wedding took place under a Chuppah, the traditional canopy under which Jewish couples are married. It gave a Jewish identity to my wedding, but the most important thing about our day was that God was there.

I can't say that my life as a follower of Yeshua has been easy. Following Yeshua is not a soft option for anyone – let alone for Jewish people – and Yeshua does not magic-away all our troubles. Also, being a follower of Yeshua does not mean that I'm perfect, far from it. It amazes me just how often I say or do or think something that is wrong in the eyes of God. It makes me realise just how unworthy I am of God's love, but I do know God's love and I know that Yeshua *is* "the Way, the Truth and the Life". I've found peace with the God of my fathers, the God of Abraham, Isaac and Jacob, through Yeshua the Messiah, the one promised by God through our prophets. In him I have the most special relationship of all.

Paying the Price

Bernard

I was born in Hackney, London, and up to the age of four I lived at Stoke Newington. My family then moved to Chingford, and along our road there were thirteen other Jewish families. The children played with each other, and my best friend was Alan Zipson. One day I would be at his house, and the next he would be at mine. We enjoyed playing Monopoly and spent hours playing a single game. We also really enjoyed playing in the street, even if we were just kicking a tennis ball against a lamp-post, although I'm not sure that the neighbours were as keen as we were!

Minyan Boy

Our home was reasonably Orthodox. We fixed mezuzot on our doors, and we all ate kosher food, except for dad. Although he was the only member of his family to marry a Jewish girl and had promised that our home would be kosher, he would not eat kosher meat and mum had to go specially to a non-kosher butcher to get meat just for him! As children we went to synagogue classes three times a week, on Tuesday and Thursday evenings after school and on Sunday mornings. We learned to read Hebrew and were taught about our festivals and the history of our people. On Sundays I also played football in the Maccabi league and attended the youth club at the synagogue hall.

On Saturdays I would go to synagogue and would sing in the choir. At thirteen I had my Bar Mitzvah and, having passed my Bar Mitzvah test with credit, I was able to read Maftir and Haftorah. I was now able to be a minyan boy. When someone dies, the male next of kin should go to the synagogue each morning to say the Kaddish (mourners' prayer) for one year after the death. A minyan of ten men is required to be able to say the prayer and, because the male congregation was less than ten, young boys who had just had their Bar Mitzvah were employed as "minyan boys". I had to go to the morning service six days a week and was paid ten shillings. If I missed a morning the Rabbi deducted two shillings and sixpence. We were not needed on the Sabbath as then we already had a minyan. The Rabbi and some of the older men used to say the Hebrew prayers as fast as they could, and the first one to finish would congratulate himself and check how long it took him, but I felt that this was not honouring to God.

We celebrated all the major festivals: Rosh HaShanah, Yom Kippur, Simchat Torah, Pesach, Purim, Hanukkah, Shavuot and Succot. At the Rosh HaShanah and Yom

Kippur services, we used to play a game. Those were the only days on which the synagogue was full; every synagogue member had their own allocated seat. The youngsters didn't have seats, so we would each take an empty seat until someone told us we were sitting in their place. We would then move to the next available space and the winner of the game was the one who could stay seated for the longest time.

At sixteen, I left school, was articled to a firm of Chartered Accountants, and for five years I signed Articles. I had always known that I would work with figures, as I was useless at science subjects, couldn't do woodwork or metalwork, and was not very good at languages. Maths was my strongest subject and I liked working with figures. A former pupil who was articled to a firm of Chartered Accountants returned to the school to announce that his firm had a vacancy. Was anyone interested? So it was that I started my first job.

I'm Jewish!

One day I was asked if I would like to go to St Luke's youth club. I already went to a youth club, but at this one they played football, something I was very keen on! The club was run by St Luke's church, and the leader was a lay reader in that church. They always spent a short while talking about the Bible and Yeshua, but as I was Jewish and we read only the Tanakh, I knew this had nothing to do with me. The club used to start with the "religious bit," so I would turn up when it was over. When they changed and had the Bible talk at the end, I would leave just as it started. When they changed yet again, and scheduled the talk at the middle, I would leave the hall until it was over and then go back in. But after a while I began to stay for the talk and would then argue with the leader about what he had said. Being Jewish, I believed that Yeshua had nothing to do with me. However, I was given John Stott's book *Basic Christianity*, and found it very interesting because it answered the kind of questions I was asking. Was Jesus the Son of God? Was he the Messiah? If it were true, what was I going to do about it?

At my Bar Mitzvah, I had to recite The Thirteen Principles of Faith. The twelfth principle was, "I believe with perfect faith in the coming of the Messiah and though he tarry I will wait daily for his coming". All Bar Mitzvah boys had to recite this. I told myself that I couldn't become a follower of Yeshua; I was Jewish and I was supposed to believe with perfect faith in the Jewish Messiah, not the Gentile Christ. However, I started to go to the evening services at St Luke's, telling my parents that I was going to a friend's house. I had been going to St Luke's for about six months when a new curate and his wife came to the church. His wife started to talk to each of the young people and asked me how long I had been a Christian. I said, "I'm not yet; I'm Jewish". "Oh yes?" she said, "So am I".

I was gobsmacked! Here was another person who had gone through what I was going through and had realised that the Gentile *Christ* was also the Jewish *Messiah*. God knew that I needed a jolt to help me make the decision to accept Yeshua as Mashiach and my Saviour. This lady had been divinely sent to help me, and I accepted Yeshua as my Saviour. However, that wasn't something Jewish people did, and I didn't know how I was going to tell my family.

Brainwashed or Belief?

The following night, when I arrived home from work, I explained to my parents that I had become a follower of Yeshua. They told me I did not know what I was talking about, that I had been brainwashed and that I was to forget all the rubbish about "that man" and the Goyim who follow him. Each night when I came home from work we would have arguments. What had they done wrong? Why had I done this to them? Many tears flowed. The atmosphere in the house was tense, and I did not enjoy being there. My parents arranged for the Rabbi to speak to me, but he said it was like talking to a brick wall. My wealthy uncle offered to send me to Israel for six months – all expenses paid – in the hope that during that time I would forget the phase I was going through. I told him he would be wasting his money, as I would find a church to go to in Israel.

Later, I told my parents of my decision to be baptised. After this, a gentleman from the courts came to see me at the office to serve me with a writ telling me that I was a Ward of Court. The official solicitor was now my legal Guardian. My minister could not baptise me and, if he did, both he and I could go to prison. I was eighteen years old, and my parents wanted me to stay a Ward of Court until I was twenty-one, hoping that in the intervening years I would forget all about Yeshua. I had to wait six months for the case to come up in court, and the situation at home continued to be tense.

Eventually the day of the court case arrived, and after the judge had heard the Barrister speak on behalf of my parents, he asked me to go with him into his private chambers. He wanted to find out if I had been brainwashed or whether I knew what I was doing. He was satisfied that I knew my own mind and awarded the case to me. My parents ordered me out of the home immediately. I had nowhere to go and no money. I went to stay with my minister for two weeks and then a widow from the church said I could live with her. She charged me a mere £3 per week to cover the cost of food.

Pushed Away

As far as my parents were concerned, I no longer existed. I didn't see them or any of my relations and only kept in touch with one sister by telephone. My mother would ask my sister if she had heard from me and how was I getting along, but I didn't see them for about eight years. At one stage, my father was involved in a very serious motor accident, and his life was hanging in the balance, but I was not allowed to visit him as they said that the shock might have killed him. However, through a friend, my parents later asked me to visit them, which I did. I started to see them on a regular basis.

When I got engaged, I asked my parents if they would like to meet my fiancée.

"Is she Jewish?" they asked.

"No," I replied.

"Why can't you marry a nice Jewish girl?" they asked. "We don't want to meet her."

My fiancée and I used to speak to each other on the telephone every day, and once when I was visiting my parents she rang up to speak to me. While we were talking, my mother said, "Why don't you invite her over?" We arranged a convenient date for her to visit, and she soon became a favourite with my father.

Initially, I had to pay a painfully high price for my discovery that the Mashiach was not just an idea in the Eighteen Benedictions, but a real person called Yeshua. He was a real Jewish man, and when I embraced him as Messiah and Lord, no pressure was going to make me turn my back on the greatest discovery of my life. Yeshua said that he did not come to divide families but because of him families would be divided. I didn't want to be cut off from my family, but they forced me out because I wouldn't deny what I knew was true. I believe that God honours those who honour him and, in my case, this resulted in restored relations with my family who had rejected me because I accepted the One who was despised and rejected.

There and Back Again

Anita

I was born in Leeds in 1937, and my mother, Rebekka, gave me a strictly Orthodox Jewish upbringing. She had emigrated with her family from a town near Riga in Latvia. They lived in the Leylands, the Jewish ghetto in Leeds at that time. It was a difficult life for the Jewish immigrants who lived there, and it was not made any easier by the Fascist Black-shirts who used to regularly beat up Jewish people on York Road.

I remember being on a tram with my mother when a woman came up to us and screamed at us, "You killed Christ!" My mother replied, "Don't be ridiculous", only to be met with a torrent of abuse, so we got off the tram at North Street. We were regularly called "dirty Jews," "Sheeneys," (see Glossary) and told to "go back to your own country." On one occasion I was crying after being called a "Sheeney" and Sally Orange, one of my mother's friends, said, "Don't cry, when they call you that, remember that it means you are a shiny star." It didn't mean that, but it made me feel better! The local park on North Street was very popular with the large Jewish community of Leeds and was soon called by most people "the Sheeney Park". We were not made to feel welcome even though I was born in Leeds.

My grandmother, who was very frum (Orthodox), once threw me out of the house for simply mentioning the name "Jesus" after hearing about him in school. I was confused, not understanding what was so wrong in saying his name; she made me stand outside for over half an hour. When I was finally let in the house she forbade me from ever saying "that name" again.

My father, Kenneth Herbert Kitchen, divorced my mother and moved to America where he became a bona fide gangster in Chicago. He was part of the Zinkle gang who were implicated in the murder of a police officer. My estranged father was deported back to England where he opened a strip club on Coburg Street in Leeds. The club was later raided and closed by the police after a tip off from my mother. After the divorce, my mother moved us all over the place and, as a child, I lived in Leeds, Cardiff, Dublin, London, Blackpool and Canada.

At the age of twelve, my traditional Jewish upbringing took a dramatic detour. I had the unusual and traumatic experience of living in a brothel. The sister of my mother's boyfriend was the "madam" or, in modern terms, the pimp who ran the brothel. I saw things no child ought to witness and was propositioned by numerous lecherous men. I hated the place!

I was not a happy child with my mother moving me

so frequently, so I often used to skip school. I was caught, and as was common in those days, taken to court and sent to a 'care home' for two weeks till the court decided what to do with me. It was not a good time for me. Finally, I was sent to live with my aunt and uncle for two years of probation. I was fourteen years old and treated like a criminal! I was treated as little more than a slave in my relatives' home, and although I was miserable, I did what I was told as they threatened to send me back to "the home" if I didn't. I cried myself to sleep every night. After two years of probation, I went to live with my mother again.

My nightmare seemed to never end, and it was only when my mother decided to move to Canada that we left England and our fortunes changed for a while. She met and fell in love with Ellis, who became the father I never had. He converted to Orthodox Judaism in order to marry my mother, and they subsequently moved to Leeds to live with my grandmother.

Sadness, trauma, and pain, however, seemed to stalk my family, and our new-found happiness didn't last long. My brother lived with my natural father but was deeply unhappy. Later in life, during a burglary on her home, my mother suffered an extremely violent attack from which she never fully recovered and was left with deep physical and emotional scars.

Truth and Despair
Over the years, I had met some kind, genuine people who loved Yeshua the Messiah, and as a result I really felt drawn towards hearing about "that name" again. Ken and Edith, a lovely Jewish couple who believed in Yeshua, took

me to hear a well-known preacher called Eric Hutchins. As he spoke, I felt I was hearing a cosmic absolute truth speaking directly to me. I felt uncomfortable and yet exhilarated at the same time. Eric said that the only way to get a new life or to be genuinely happy was through Yeshua the Messiah. There and then I was absolutely convinced of the truth of what he was saying; I turned my back on despair and accepted Yeshua into my life as my Messiah and Lord. The fact that I was Jewish with an Orthodox upbringing did not cause me a moment of hesitation; I was just gripped by the truth of who Yeshua was in history and who he was at that moment for me as a Jewish woman.

Several years later, my dear brother killed himself. He had seemed unable to ever feel happy and suffered terrible depression. I could not understand why my brother had been allowed to die, and I turned from God. I was so angry with God that I even threw my Bible across the room, and for many years I blamed him for what had happened. Six years later, my natural father killed himself, so once again I was thrown into deep despair and agony. My mother developed cancer and I nursed her through it. Many other problems arose, but my new friends who loved "that name" never deserted me.

Back Again

After many years of anger and doubt, a dear friend called Helen invited me to go to a local Messianic Fellowship with her. There I met other Jewish people who loved and followed Yeshua as their Messiah and Lord. As I attended those meetings, I began to open my heart and ask God to forgive me for all the years of rebellion and doubt. When the fog of pain, doubt, bitterness and confusion lifted, I finally saw that God had always been in the background caring for me; I had just been too blinded by anger to see it. I am now at a place in my life where I ask myself how I could have ever doubted his undying love for me. I always felt like someone was watching over me through all the experiences of my life, and it was not by chance that there were always people who have been good to me "in that name" in the darkest times. My life was destroyed by two selfish people, my parents, but restored by the most unselfish person, the rabbi from Nazareth.

I have a wonderful, caring husband who has stood by my side through it all and who has looked after me when I have been ill. I also have three lovely daughters, grandchildren and great-grandchildren; I thank God each day for giving me so many blessings. Life still throws up challenges and pain; the difference now is that instead of becoming angry, despairing and blaming God, I turn to him for the strength he promises. I know that his strength will get me through when my own fails. I proved this to be true when I had an operation on my thyroid gland; and also when I was dealing with the deep sadness brought about by the death of Ellis, who was more of a real, loving father than my genetic father ever was. Both my fathers are gone, but I am so grateful that I have a heavenly Father who will never leave me nor forsake me, even if I sometimes feel like I want to forsake him.

From Pain to Peace

Esme

I was born in 1926 and brought up in a Jewish family in the north of England. My parents were not all that observant, going to synagogue only on Yom Kippur. My father, who was a tailor, spent more time in the pub than the synagogue! However, we did keep Shabbat and Passover. We lived in the Jewish neighbourhood till I was nine, but we were not very strict in keeping all the laws of Judaism. Benjamin, my father, was born in Minsk, Belarus, and at the age of ten came to Leeds, where his uncle had a clothing business. My mother Jenny was born in Leeds, but her mother was born in Poland. We weren't a very close or loving family; my parents were totally focused on living their own lives as opposed to a family life, and I was pretty much ignored and left to my own devices. I was what is known as a "latchkey child"; the key to our home was left under a large seashell at the back door so I could let myself in after school. My mother always told me to look after the house, but she never told me to look after myself. My parents never really encouraged me in anything I did, and as a consequence, I became very withdrawn.

Schoolyard Anti-Semitism

After moving house, we lived in a non-Jewish area, and at school I was the only Jewish child in the class. Before the other children knew I was Jewish, I got on well with them all; they had no reason not to like me. However, when they found out that I was Jewish, everything changed and the trauma began. The Catholic children would often repeat what their parents said about me: "She killed our Lord". Their parents had forbidden them to play with "the Christ-killer"; that was me! I was often beaten and pushed around in the schoolyard. It was a game for them, but for me it was terrifying, and I used to skip school to avoid this racist abuse.

Break-up and Breakdown

My life has been full of pain; my first husband was Jewish and abusive. My second husband was a Gentile and was much worse, in fact very violent. For some strange psychological reason, I always blamed myself for the bad things that happened to me. Like most victims of different forms of serial cruelty, I had a low self-image and looked for the fault in myself instead of facing the fact that I was a victim of abuse. Despite the pain, God blessed me with a son and a daughter by my first husband, who was extremely bitter about our separation and wouldn't let me see the children. This resulted in me having a serious nervous breakdown.

For many years the only God consciousness in my life was when, in times of need, I cried out: "God help me!" Little did I realise that Someone was listening to my cries of desperation, let alone willing to answer them.

New Covenant Child

Many years later I started up a senior citizens' social club, and it was there that I met my close friend Doreen, who had begun to attend after her husband died. Shortly after that, Doreen began to go along to her local church. I was fascinated. I asked her, "What is a vicar like?"

I went to Doreen's church purely out of curiosity and met her vicar. I sat asking him questions in his home till midnight and was given the book *Child of the Covenant* by Michele Guinness, a Jewish woman who believed in Yeshua. I read it avidly and as I read I heard a voice in my head, which said, "You also are a child of the New Covenant." I felt honoured and thrilled.

Peter the vicar invited me to an Easter service. There was a wooden cross lying on the floor, and I felt moved as I looked at it while the minister was explaining how Yeshua suffered at the crucifixion. I was imagining the punishment Yeshua bore for me and for the whole world.

I visualized Yeshua carrying the cross. I didn't even know at the time that I was a sinner because Jewish people are not taught that! I thought how heavy that cross must have been if it carried the sin of the whole world, and I started to cry as I realised it was my fault that Yeshua had gone to the cross. I kept repeating, "I'm sorry! I'm sorry!" The text of Peter's sermon that morning was John 3:16: "For God so loved the world that He gave his only Son that whosoever believes in Him should not perish but should have everlasting life." The sermon greatly comforted me and gave me real peace but, for weeks afterwards, every time I thought of the cross of Yeshua, I wept.

Forgiven to Forgive

I was greatly challenged by the teaching of forgiveness in Mark 11:24-25:

> Everything you ask for in prayer will be yours, if you only have faith. Whenever you stand up to pray, you must forgive what others have done to you. Then your Father in heaven will forgive your sins.

If God had forgiven me, I should also forgive all who had hurt me. This I did after a struggle, and I received great peace. I prayed that the Lord would bring my own children back into my life, and he answered my prayers through a variety of circumstances and providences.

Going and growing

In the local parish church I was attending, there was not much Bible teaching so I did not grow spiritually. One day whilst out shopping, we saw some people finishing an open-air meeting. I asked two women what it was all about, and after we chatted they prayed for my arthritis and I felt some relief. Within three months the pain had gone and has never returned.

As a result, I started to attend a local congregation, and on 8th December 1996 I was immersed in water as a believer in Yeshua. The much misunderstood baptism, coming from the Jewish Mikvah ceremony, is a symbol that my sins (but not my Jewish identity!) are washed away. God created me a Jew, and he doesn't want to change that. Yeshua died for me, a Jewish woman. Yeshua was unashamedly a Jew, so being Jewish and a follower of Yeshua is not a source of shame or pain for me either.

Some years ago, someone introduced me to the leader of the local Messianic Fellowship, and Doreen and I have attended regularly ever since. It was there that, for the first time since my childhood, I celebrated Passover, and now all the Jewish festivals and my Jewish identity have such extra meaning and power.

From Russia With Love!

Sonya

I was born and brought up in a Jewish family in the city of St. Petersburg (Leningrad), Russia. My parents were both survivors of the notorious German blockade of the city during World War II. My parents never spoke about us being Jewish in my early years, and to my surprise I discovered I was Jewish at the age of seven when I was told so at school. Being Jewish in the former Soviet era was, to say the least, not a great advantage. I had to always work twice as hard to prove I was as good as the other pupils. Discrimination against Jewish people was accepted as the norm, and as Israel is a Jewish State, it was not favoured when it regularly appeared in the news. Even back then, in our political news lessons Israel was always portrayed as the eternally guilty Western-backed bourgeoisie aggressor against the proletariat Palestinians. When Israel was mentioned in class, the teacher would often focus on me, giving me a withering look as if I was personally to blame.

Our family was a typical secular, non-observant, Soviet Jewish family. We celebrated some of the Jewish festivals and, for me, being Jewish was more of a burden than a joy. The only reminder that I was Jewish was when my Mum used to buy Matzah (unleavened bread) every year around Passover time, or when my teacher gave me one of those looks. Occasionally my mother used to prepare Jewish dishes like Tsimess, Kneidalach, Farshmak, Gefiltefish and many more wonderful dishes.

This "God Business"

In my late teens and early twenties, I was greatly involved in astrology and the occult, which took me far away from God and actually created an "anti-God" feeling inside me. My mum came to faith in Yeshua through a public religious meeting in Russia in 1990. Her life changed completely, and she began to host Bible studies in our flat. Although I did not actively participate in the meetings, I started meeting believers in Yeshua who used to attend. In principle, I was very much against their faith in Yeshua and this "God business", and I truly believed that my mum had gone mad. One day in late 1994, a meeting was held in our home and, as usual, I was sitting in the kitchen waiting for it to finish so I could watch television. The meeting was coming to an end, and during the public prayer I became impatient and laughed sarcastically in my heart at these "silly people" who were praying. Immediately after those thoughts had gone through my mind, I felt a sharp pain as though a sword were slicing through my flesh. I understood that I might have offended God (whom I did not believe existed until that moment) by these thoughts, and I asked his forgiveness. To my shock and surprise, the pain immediately disappeared!

A Cup of Forgiveness

When the meeting finished and people were preparing to go home, I noticed that one lady was looking at me, but I did not pay too much attention. This was the first time this lady had attended the meeting in our house. She was invited by a friend but did not know my mum. A few weeks later the same lady, Vala, turned up again at our home, and, surprisingly for me, I offered her a cup of tea. What was even more unusual was that I invited Vala into my room, where our conversation revolved around God and Yeshua. Eventually we came to the point where Vala asked me whether I wanted my sins to be forgiven. I surprised myself even more by responding positively and getting on my knees and praying with true intent in my heart to receive forgiveness from Yeshua my Messiah. My thirst for forgiveness amazed even me and was certainly an act of God. I felt a great sense of relief, as though a big burden had been lifted. My heart was filled with great joy, and I suddenly was proud and not afraid to be a Jew.

I felt a great desire to share my new discovery with as many people as I could. Up to this point, perhaps as a result of the Soviet anti-Israel education, I had always been indifferent to the state of Israel, but suddenly and mysteriously my heart was filled with love and affection for the land of my fathers and where Yeshua lived. I wanted to go there and see it with my own eyes.

Pride in the Name

Being brought up in the Soviet Union under a Communist and atheistic system didn't encourage a sense of Jewish pride to develop in me naturally. Because of my love of Yeshua, the Messiah of Israel, I suddenly felt I was truly Jewish, and for the first time in my life I felt great pride in my Jewishness, something I never imagined I would ever feel.

In 1996 I made Aliyah (immigration) to Israel with my family, and there I attended a congregation of Messianic Jews in a town south of Tel Aviv. Finding such a good congregation was a great blessing from God as I was so young in the faith. In late 2000, I married my husband Gil and moved to Britain with him. We now have two daughters, Emma and Hannah. Strangely enough, after we moved to Britain, a respected member of a congregation we were attending told me that I was no longer Jewish! I was deeply offended and hurt by that. The fact is that I am more consciously Jewish and proud of that fact than I have ever been in my life.

My life as a Jewish believer in Yeshua in Britain is no less Jewish than it was in Israel; more than that, I'm unashamed and unapologetic of my discovery that Yeshua is our promised Messiah, despite the fact that the religious authorities in Israel would seek to strip my Jewish identity away. I believe it is true, and I won't be bullied by anyone into saying otherwise. I had enough of that under Soviet Communism! In our family, we have strong awareness of our identity as Jews and our strong links with Israel. This does not in any way put a barrier between us and Yeshua; in fact, it is a natural as breathing.

Desperately Seeking Truth

Gil

What I am about to tell you is quite amazing. Even now, I still find it difficult to grasp the sequence of events that transformed my life. Here is my story.

My name is Gil (which in Hebrew means "joy"). I was born into a secular middle-class family in Haifa, Israel, in 1963. My parents were of Eastern European Jewish origin, but I was raised as a secular Israeli. Being Jewish for me meant "traditions". At school we studied the Bible as an historical book, mainly to know and understand the history and traditions of our people, but, as far as I was concerned, God was an abstract being that existed only in Bible stories. We all hated the Bible classes since, for us, they were boring history lessons with no spiritual content.

That Name

My parents had never been religious, but they respected traditional values. At home we hardly kept any holidays, not even Yom Kippur, the Day of Atonement, which is considered very holy even by non-religious people. My dad was a coach driver and tourist guide, and in my childhood I used to travel with him a lot to the various places where Yeshua walked. But although I heard about Yeshua, I knew little more about him than that he was born in Bethlehem.

One day, during one of our Bible lessons at school, the teacher was talking about the book of Micah chapter 5:

> Now gather yourself in troops, O daughter of troops;
> He has laid siege against us; they will strike the judge
> of Israel with a rod on the cheek. But you, Bethlehem
> Ephrathah, though you are little among the thousands
> of Judah, yet out of you shall come forth to Me the One
> to be Ruler in Israel, Whose goings forth are from of old,
> from everlasting.

Because I knew Yeshua had been born in Bethlehem, it immediately sprang into my mind: "This must be about Yeshua!" I raised my hand and told the teacher and the class with confidence that this passage talks about Yeshua. The teacher's response was very harsh, and I was almost thrown out of the class for even mentioning "that name".

Seeking Enlightenment

Like all Israelis, I had to do three years of compulsory military service, and in the 1982 Lebanon War, my unit was deployed around the city of Beirut. I trained as an officer and signed on for an additional two years. In the latter part of my service, I worked as a computer programmer in the Tel Aviv area. At that time I was searching for God but, because I could not see a path to God in Judaism, I read a lot about Eastern philosophies, especially Buddhism and Hinduism.

In 1985, while still on active service, I became ill with iron deficiency anaemia, and after two years of seeking a cure through conventional medicine, I turned to alternative medicine. To the amazement of the doctors, I recovered! This almost miraculous cure convinced me to research alternative medicine, and after I left the army in 1987, I chose to study acupuncture in England.

In my last years at school, I had had private English tuition from a lady I deeply respected, and before I left Israel, I visited her. She told me that she believed Yeshua was the Messiah and gave me some advice: "Gil, you are about to go to a foreign country and may come across many difficulties but, whenever you are in trouble or need support, ask God to help you in the name of Yeshua and wonderful things will happen in your life." Her words became very precious and valuable to me in the years to come.

The Invisible Hand

In England I studied in East Grinstead in the beautiful county of West Sussex, and my studies included Chinese philosophy, particularly Taoism. I discovered that Eastern philosophers talk about a spiritual experience or enlightenment which, when achieved, brings us as close as possible to knowing the "Ultimate" or "Source of all things". This kind of "Force" is not personal and does not exercise moral judgement. However, in spite of my studies and my New Age activities, I could not find fulfilment, and God seemed to be further away than ever. Nevertheless, there always seemed to be an invisible hand helping me, and every time I was about to give up and go back to Israel, things happened to change my circumstances for the better. I could actually feel that "Someone" was looking after me, and that there was a purpose in my struggle, although at the time I could have never even dreamt who that somebody or purpose was.

In the summer of 1990, I moved house and started my own acupuncture practice, but within a few months, things started to go very wrong; I did not have enough patients and I was in deep debt. In my despair, I decided to return to computer programming and contacted various professional computer recruitment agencies, but, because I didn't have a full permit to work in the United Kingdom, none of them would help me. I felt that there was no way out for me, and my despair deepened.

Once is happenstance...
One night in early December 1990, I lay in bed thinking about the words of my English teacher: "Whenever you are in trouble or need support, ask God to help you in the name of Yeshua and wonderful things will happen." Could this be true? Nothing else seemed to work, so I decided to give it a try and called to him in my heart: "God, if you are there, please help me in this difficult time. In the name of Yeshua." Without thinking much about what I had done, I went to sleep. A few days later, a recruitment agency called to say they were interested in my technical skills and experience. I thought that

because of the problem with my work permit they would not contact me again but within minutes they called to say that their client was willing to issue the required permit. Within four months, I had repaid all my debts and had a company car. However, at the time, this sudden change in my life after praying "in the name of Yeshua" all seemed to be just coincidence.

After eighteen months, at the height of the recession in the early nineties, the company was in great trouble and had serious problems obtaining a work permit for me. However, I thought my job was secure and bought a new house. After moving into it, I returned to the office to be told that I no longer had a job. It felt like everything was crumbling again. I was back to "square one" with no job and no permanent work permit; but now I had a mortgage to pay. Having no work permit during a recession, there seemed no way out.

Twice is coincidence...
The advice of my English teacher came back to me, and again I asked God to help me in the name of Yeshua. I did not expect an answer, but after a few days the impossible happened. A recruitment agency called to say that British Airways wanted to interview me. The interview was a success, and my work permit was eventually issued. However, I still refused to believe that this was an answer to my prayer. In my mind, it was just another lucky coincidence.

During the next couple of years, I was involved in a number of key projects within British Airways and found myself in central positions where my technical advice and knowledge were required. By the end of

1994, my work permit needed to be renewed; normally it is very difficult to obtain such an extension. My first application was rejected, and the situation again seemed very bleak. It looked as though I was about to lose everything.

One evening, a friend came to see me, and as we talked about life and various philosophical viewpoints, the conversation moved to Yeshua. I believed that Yeshua was a very special person, but I could not see the relevance of events that happened two thousand years ago to our lives today. My friend remarked: "Why don't you ask God to show you that Yeshua is the truth?" His words echoed in my mind. I tried to get them out of my head, but as I lay in bed that night I said: "O God, I have all these problems with my work permit, please show me that Yeshua is the truth and help me to solve this problem."

Three times is...
The very next morning, the office phone rang and I heard the voice of my agent: "Gil, I have good news for you. We have just received your work permit for another three years." I was overcome with joy and shocked from the obvious connection to the request I made the night before. For the first time, I saw a definite connection between my plea to God and the answer.

Everything in my life now seemed fine. I had a good job, plenty of money, a new car and a nice house, but I did not feel at peace in my heart. I still felt the need to find God. I talked to my friend and his Israeli wife, who showed me very convincing reasons for believing that Yeshua was the Messiah. I suddenly had the strange feeling that maybe this was the truth.

But it couldn't be that simple, I thought. How could I, as a Jew, believe in Yeshua? As if to answer my unspoken questions, my friend's wife handed me the book *Betrayed* by Stan Telchin. She had offered me this story of an American Jewish family who believed Yeshua was the Messiah several times before, but each time I had firmly refused. This time, however, I heard myself say I would accept it.

Not So Good

A week later, I started reading *Betrayed* and did not put it down until I had finished the last page. I was fascinated, but I was afraid to give myself to him and simply thought that there was no other response needed apart from accepting the historical fact that Yeshua was the promised Messiah. I started to feel very uncomfortable with myself. I had visions from the past of all the things I had gone through and all the dreams I had as a kid about making a difference in the world. I started to realise that I was not such a good person after all and that I had treated many people badly.

One day, I felt I needed to get hold of a Bible, but immediately pushed the thought out of my mind, wondering why I should have such a strange idea. Later that month, a friend called to say she had met a nice Israeli girl called Sarah, who would like to meet me. She commented that Sarah believed in Yeshua. I didn't care because I thought everybody was entitled to their own beliefs, but, when I met her, she talked most of the evening about Yeshua and her faith. I felt as though Yeshua was chasing me. "Why is this happening to me!" I thought.

Haunted

During the following week, I contacted Sarah, and in one of our phone conversations she kept mentioning her faith in Yeshua. I felt really fed up talking to her and was about to slam the phone down when a sharp thought – almost like someone was speaking to me – came into my mind:"Just listen to her!" I was startled. It felt like I was frozen and could not put the phone down.

It was Friday, and I felt very tired after a whole week of hectic conversations. I was very depressed as it looked like things were not going very well for me. Again, I felt haunted by many things in my past that seemed to be incomplete, especially by the way I had treated people and how I had not always been totally honest in my relationships. At the time, I did not realise that God was convicting me of my past sins. I also started to think about what would happen to me after death. Most of my beliefs were based on the New Age concepts, so I thought that we all probably came back for another chance after we died. During that week, all these foundations had started to shake, and I remember thinking that maybe death was final. What would happen to me? Would I be with God? I felt no certainty of that and began to realise that I might end up in eternal darkness away from God with all the wrong and incomplete things from my past surrounding me. In terror I thought, "No, this cannot be true". But I felt a great need for forgiveness.

From Minus to Plus

Around noon that Friday, I called on my friends who gave me *Betrayed*. I always felt there was something special about them, as they were always welcoming to guests and would see anybody at any time. I recognised a kind of peace in their behaviour, As we discussed God and Yeshua, I felt something happening inside me, and I wanted to go home to be on my own.

At home, it felt like my life was crumbling around me. I picked up a booklet called *From Minus to Plus* that had been posted through my door two years earlier. Reading through it, I decided to say the prayer at the back of the booklet, but when I did nothing "happened." So, I decided to go to bed and sleep everything away. However, I couldn't sleep. I felt a great need to come to God. I remember the great need for forgiveness I felt at the time, and I truly wanted to start anew. I also realised that Yeshua had died for me, and in my mind I could see him on the cross. I started to plead with God from the heart: "O God, please forgive me for all the wrong I have done and the way I have treated people in the past. Please take me; I give myself to you completely". Then I asked God to accept my plea "in the name of Yeshua".

The next thing I remember was that I sensed a kind of a wave or wind descending on me and going through me. I felt as though a huge, heavy stone had been removed from me, and a peace and love that I had never experienced before surrounded me. I felt the presence of Yeshua around me. I knew that Yeshua was the Truth and, although I had not read the Tanakh for fifteen years and had not read the New Testament at all, at that point I "knew" that the Bible was the Word of God. I could feel his pain, suffering for me, and I wept quietly, thanking Yeshua for looking after me all those years, for leading me to himself and for saving me. Suddenly, I wanted to know more about him and almost instantly the "answer" came into my mind: "Read the New Covenant."

Amazing Grace

A few minutes later, surrounded by his love and serenity, I fell asleep. After one of the most peaceful nights I can recall, I woke up feeling completely different. It was as though I was not the same person anymore. I had a very strong urge to get a Bible, and then my mind moved to various issues and beliefs that I had held for years, which suddenly looked so wrong. I felt like a new person, and my heart was full of love, peace and joy. I knew nothing about the "New Birth". All I realised at the time was that Yeshua was the Truth, and the Bible was the Word of God. The first thing I did that morning was to get a Bible and then go to see my friends who, after hearing the news, rejoiced in amazement.

I can only say that coming to know Yeshua was the most important event of my life, and his joy and peace are with me every day wherever I go. I am grateful to the Lord for all he has done for me, and I wish my life to be dedicated to him, that whatever I do or whatever path I take may be for his ultimate glory and purpose.

I will always feel touched by words of John Newton, which speak so much to me:

Amazing grace! How sweet the sound
That saved a wretch like me.
I once was lost, but now am found,
Was blind, but now I see.
'Twas grace that taught my heart to fear,
And grace my fears relieved.
How precious did that grace appear
The hour I first believed.

Somebody Knocking On My Door

Lynda

I was born in Cambridge in 1955 to a secular British Jewish mother. My father was an American with some Christianity in his background, but I'm not sure whether he called himself a Christian out of conviction or simply because Christianity was America's national religion. I was a premature baby, and, because I have cerebral palsy, I did not walk until I was five years old. Several of my mother's relatives on her father's side were strongly into false religions, notably Christian Science and Baba worship, a form of Hinduism and New Age religion. Our Christian Scientist relatives persuaded my parents that my disability was an illusion and that I would be healed if they did what the Christian Scientist church taught and said the necessary prayers. Needless to say, this was a lie, and it probably had some sort of anaesthetising effect on my parents that prevented them from ever looking to God.

I was brought up with a strong awareness that I was Jewish, but I had very little understanding of what it really meant to be Jewish. Because services at the local Orthodox synagogue were conducted solely in Hebrew and we didn't know Hebrew, we didn't attend. However, I do remember observing Friday night Kabbalat Shabbat until I was ten and being taught to pray Psalms 23 and 121. At the age of ten I was sent to a Hebrew school, or cheder, for the first time, but it was deeply embarrassing because even the younger children were miles ahead of me in their studies!

Our Friend, Yeshua

I was incredibly shy, but my sister was the opposite; she was a real socialite. My mother pleaded with me to make friends, but I was more of a bookworm and lacked confidence. I felt that people didn't really like me. However, one day I was invited to an event for sixth formers that turned out to be a Bible study on the book of Revelation, in particular the passage where Yeshua said that he would spit us out of his mouth if we were lukewarm (Rev. 3:16). I remember praying fervently that I might be "hot" and not "lukewarm".

The next week, there was a youth group event at which there was a speaker. I was invited to go and went partly, I'm sure, to get my mum off my back, but I felt much loved by those I met there. There was a certain something about them that I warmed to. The talk was about *Someone* standing at a door and knocking. Because others were taking notes, I did the same and still have my journal from that time. The speaker explained that this *Someone* was Yeshua and that he wanted to be our friend. Naive though it seems now, I had no idea that, traditionally, as a Jewish person, I wasn't supposed to even mention the name of Yeshua. I had never heard this teaching and assumed my parents hadn't either, but I was quite sure that I wanted the friendship of Yeshua. The speaker must have explained sin and the meaning of the cross, but I didn't understand any of that. What I did understand was that Yeshua wanted to be in my life and so, on 23rd September 1973, I asked him to come into my life. The result was that God – in whom I had always believed and to whom I had written in a previous journal entry: "Please God make something happen!" – was no longer "up there somewhere"; he was now close to me.

Shock and Pain

I would not recommend that any other person do what I did that night after the meeting; I went back home really excited and read the whole sermon back to my parents, who were in bed! Their reaction was a shock to me and pretty painful, but I went back to my room and prayed again.

I can truly say that in the years since that evening, even though my parents were negative towards my faith in Yeshua, the Lord has been my shepherd. The girl who invited me to the meetings had parents who were real disciples of Yeshua, but she had only just come to faith herself. Week by week she supplied me with real solid spiritual classics that established me in my new-found faith.

A Firm Foundation

I had the opportunity to take a year out before university and visited Mexico. The year out – which took me away from home and the displeasure of my parents – and a strong fellowship in York were terrifically helpful in enabling me to grow spiritually. As the Lord gave me a community of such loving acceptance in the fellowship and on the university campus, I thought I had arrived in heaven. They were a real family to me. A lot of emotional healing happened during that time so that, amazingly, the terrified, insecure person I had been became someone who was confident and able to sing solos in worship. I have changed a lot because, as the New Testament says, Yeshua "first loved me".

Leicester is Jerusalem!
To the outsider, the following years may have looked horribly sad and pointless, because I suddenly had a number of new health problems to struggle with. However, God promises that "all things work together for good to those who love him" and I can say with certainty that in spite of the pain during that time, there was also much blessing. I do not regret travelling the path along which I have been taken.

Having moved from York, I had started attending a fairly large evangelical Anglican church in Leicester. I believe that I was led there to receive prayer for healing, but this was not straightforward and sometimes things got worse. Yet God is faithful and wanted me to learn that my Jewishness was still significant to him and that he had plans for my life that sadly, because of that particular church's theology, I was never likely to learn there. If pressed, the Vicar would say that Leicester was our "Jerusalem" and that we were all "Israel".

Talking to Yeshua

Over time, and not without pain and struggle, God himself opened my eyes to the things written in the Bible about the Jewish people being a nation with a specific destiny. The British Messianic Jewish Alliance conferences were really important events for me. Also, I went to visit Israel and joined a group who prayed for Israel. Then God did something amazing! I was attending a church with a congregation of over 200 when, towards the end of one of the services, an Israeli couple walked in because they liked the music. The lady later told me that she had been moved to tears by watching me worship. When it was discovered where they were from, they were directed to me because I had been to Israel.

At that time I had had a wonderful gift of being able to attend weekly Hebrew lessons with a Gentile believer, so I tried out my Hebrew. The lady responded by asking if I was Jewish. Expecting a similar reaction to the one I had received from my family, I admitted hesitantly that I was.

"What are you doing here?"

"These people believe in Messiah Yeshua and so do I."

Instead of reacting negatively, the lady just said, "Oh fine!"

The lady and her husband were not believers in Yeshua. The lady was Orthodox, and her husband was an atheist and very secular. I panicked before God. Ostensibly, I had failed to convince my family of the truth about Yeshua, and I was scared because God had suddenly given me another great responsibility, to be a witness to these precious people. What could I do? God graciously showed me that I should pray for them and over the next three years, while the husband studied for a law degree and as they had their first child, our friendship developed and deepened. I have seen many answers to prayer since becoming a follower of Yeshua, but during those three years the answers were spectacular. As the Lord answered my prayers for them so quickly and specifically, they came to realise that I "talked to Yeshua about things" and asked me to pray they might find a flat in a specific area. They not only got the flat in that area but also received furniture – all from different sources – that matched perfectly.

When the husband asked me to pray for his finals, I shared with him that when I was studying 18th Century Literature, I suffered a mental block and couldn't do any revision except read three term-time essays I'd written on the subject. My exam paper could have carried any number of questions but there were three questions on exactly the areas I'd covered in my essays! The same happened for him! Many years later, we still see one another for a couple of days each year and God has continued to work in their lives. The wife has even phoned a mutual friend to ask if she would take her to a local messianic congregation I had told her about!

The Children of Abraham
God has done another amazing thing. He moved me from the church I had attended for over twenty years to a small fellowship in a very Asian area of town because of my desire to have a fellowship to which I could take a Muslim neighbour. The Muslim vanished, but God again brought an Israeli to me! This friend and her two sons have stayed in this country, and two of them are now

strong believers in Yeshua. We have a pastor who spent seven years in Israel, and his wife has Jewish ancestors who lived in Israel for thirteen years. The Gentile leaders in our church have always had a great understanding of and a burden for Israel, and celebrate the feasts. But a new impetus has come in through the recent addition of Jewish believers to the fellowship. Even Muslims walk into the church and, although language is a barrier, they know that "Something" is there.

I could never have planned the things in which God has involved me, but, in spite of all I have been through, he has been faithful.

From Hamburg by Kindertransport

Ruth

I was born in Hamburg; I'm a Hamburger! I was brought up as an ordinary German child and wasn't aware that I was different from anyone else until the age of eight when I was playing with my friends. As we were having a little quarrel, an irate woman came up and called me "a dirty little Jew". I didn't know what she meant. Not only was my home known to be very clean, but also I didn't know what a "Jew" was. However, from that point on I realised I was different from other children.

I went to a normal German school but in 1933, after Hitler came to power, the other children started to sing Nazi songs in the playground. I couldn't join in with them, and very soon I became an outcast; the other children were not allowed to play with me. Soon I had to go to a Jewish school, so we moved house.

The infamous *Kristallnacht* was on 9th November

1938. I was 13 at the time, and I slept through it! The next day I heard about Jews being dragged off and beaten up, Jewish shops being plundered, their windows broken and everything thrown into the streets. I heard about synagogues being burned, including one that I used to attend with my friends (my parents did not go to synagogue). My father decided it was time for us to get out of the country. We had tried once before, but other countries wouldn't let us in and Hitler wouldn't let us out. My father put our name down to go to British Mandate of Palestine, but my mother refused to go because of the unrest there – a decision that cost them their lives. Meanwhile, we had to endure insults and were often evicted from restaurants, which were not allowed to serve Jews.

Escape from Germany

My brother was nearly eighteen, so he and I got out very quickly after my father put our names down for the *Kindertransport*. Though we could have gone to Holland, I insisted on going to England. The Lord certainly sent us to the right country! We had about a week to sew our names into our clothing, and then my parents took us to the station and put us on the train. Little did I know that this was to be the last time I would see them as they never left Germany and were deported to a Concentration Camp by the Nazis. I settled in England, and because my foster father wouldn't let me speak German, I stopped speaking it altogether and became thoroughly assimilated into the English way of life. I even wrote to my parents in English, although I knew they would have to get the letters translated! It was a Christian home, and because I had not come from an observant Jewish home, I became used to going to church and being a "Christian".

One day in September 1939, my foster father told me that Britain had declared war on Germany. I replied that when I was old enough I would join the British army to get my own back on Hitler. I was fourteen at the time, but four years later I joined the British forces. There I met a British soldier; we got married and had children.

At the age of thirty-three, I became aware that I needed something more in my life than what I had. I started searching, and thought back to Sundays in the old days, when we would go to church, go home and have a nice lunch, go out for a walk and then end up in the parlour singing hymns. I thought of this whenever I was unhappy and in need.

I started to go to church again after a friend shared the gospel with me and became involved with the Brethren, where I received good Bible teaching. A group of us had a vision of building a new congregation on a housing estate and, after a couple of years, we left the Brethren and began meeting in a house. After saving up and buying some land, we gradually built a new place of worship. I taught Sunday school and was very involved in the congregation's life.

For many years I had little contact with my own people as there was no Jewish community where I lived. However, when I was 56, after my first husband had died, I re-learnt German and I enrolled at evening classes. The language came back easily, but little did I know that the Lord was preparing me to go back to Germany – the last place I would have wanted to go to!

Return to Germany

After living in England for fifty years, I suddenly had a niggling feeling that I should go back to Hamburg to testify of my faith in Yeshua. I didn't want to go, but the feeling would not leave me.

Some time later, my second husband and I were on holiday in Majorca, where we met two German ladies. I mentioned quite casually that I had been born in Hamburg, and that I wouldn't mind seeing what the place looked like now. I bargained with the Lord and told him I would go if I was invited by a German Christian family who loved Jews. This was an impossible condition for God to meet – or so I thought!

Three weeks later, a letter with a Hamburg postmark arrived, inviting me to visit the city. The invitation came from a German couple, and we corresponded by letter for a time before I went. My husband was by this time suffering from Alzheimer's disease, but our hosts did not mind. We stayed for two weeks and it was a very emotional journey, seeing all my old haunts, such as the school (now a museum) where a board listed the names of teachers and pupils who had been taken away in 1942, never to return, and I reflected that one of those names could have been mine. However, I knew I had to forgive the Germans – despite having never met anyone else who had been able to do this – and I knew it could only be done with the Lord's help.

I was taken to a big church in the centre of Hamburg. There, in front of about 1,500 people, I gave my testimony and told the congregation that I forgave the Germans for what they had done to my family and my people. The

Holy Spirit was present and many in the congregation were touched and after the service came to ask for my forgiveness for them personally. It was a special time.

I visited my father's old work-place and went back to see the house where I used to live. There were three old ladies sitting on a bench outside the house, and when I told them I had lived there fifty years previously, one of the ladies said she recognised my maiden name. She had been our neighbour and told me a little about my parents and how she used to try to help my mother by supplying bits of food. I wasn't sure whether to believe her or not, since many Germans are still largely unable to face up to what was done to the Jews.

All this helped me to rediscover my roots and identity. My foster-sister, however, can't understand why I still want to identify myself as a Jew!

Some Christian friends in Hamburg used to meet to pray for Israel, and the Lord called me to start a Prayer for Israel group in Oswestry, where I now live. We have a large group, but at first I didn't know how to run it. However, the Lord reminded me that my Jewish friends in Hamburg used to invite me for Shabbat. We started a little Shabbat service in Oswestry, which still continues.

In 1994, after having been back to Hamburg a couple more times, I felt I had to go to Auschwitz even though, again, I didn't want to. A German friend put my name down for a Journey of Reconciliation trip with all expenses paid, which I took as a sign from God that I was meant to go. We all met up from different parts of Germany and a German pastor led the group, which consisted of about fifty Christians and two Jews: me and the pastor of a Messianic Fellowship. During the trip we stopped at various places and had services of reconciliation, but I never quite knew which side I was on!

The Holocaust: An Act of Satan

The Holocaust was part of the devil's fight against God's plan of salvation. There were several attempted annihilations of Jewish people before the one in Germany. The first was devised by Pharaoh at the time of the Exodus; then there was Haman's "Final Solution" recorded in the Book of Esther, followed by Herod's slaughter of the Jewish children in Bethlehem. I believe very much that Satan was behind the Roman murder of Yeshua. After his resurrection, Yeshua revealed that he would return to the Jewish nation (Acts 1). In order to prevent this, the devil has tried to destroy the Jewish people, and we have suffered much persecution in every nation, culminating in the Holocaust in Germany. This repeated attempt to destroy the Jewish people is part of the spiritual battle between Satan and God.

The Journey of Reconciliation was very emotional. At Auschwitz I went on "autopilot" as I saw the sign over the gate, *Arbeit macht frei* (Work makes you free); the Germans wanted to work the Jews to death! I had tried, like so many others, to blot all this from my mind, but for the first time it came home to me who I was, and, for the first time, I cried about it. Auschwitz is now a museum, and I looked among the suitcases for one with my parents' names on it, but there wasn't one. I saw various personal possessions and hair that had been cut off. I saw a wall against which people had been put to be shot. It was horrendous. We had a memorial service for my parents, during which I cried and felt an emotional burden fall from my shoulders. My parents had been laid to rest.

When people ask me where God was when the

Holocaust was taking place, I tell them that, as I was walking round Auschwitz, I felt God reveal to me that Yeshua had been there suffering with my people.

Early the next morning, I felt I heard God tell me that all the love which had been showered on me was for him and for his people Israel; it made me feel humble and privileged to have been allowed to go on that journey. I picked up some nails from the railway because they reminded me of the nails that Yeshua had endured, when he suffered that terrible act of anti-Semitism and took the suffering of the world on to his own body. I will never forget the love of those other visitors, all of them German Christians. They brought inner healing to my soul.

I think it is important to tell young people about the Holocaust, so that it never happens again.

They Drink Blood!

Rita

I was born in the USSR in 1976. At the age of nine I heard some school friends talking about "the Jews" who drank the blood of children. When I asked my father if he'd heard of these people, he started to laugh and rocked back and forth in his seat: "Sweetheart, you are one of them; we're Jewish!" Until that point, my parents had concealed our Jewish identity for fear of persecution. My grandmother used to speak a language that I didn't recognise – it was all very mysterious. Only later did I learn that it was Yiddish, the language of European Jews which is a mix of German and Hebrew.

Stalin's Sweets
At the tender age of twelve, I heard another word for the first time, and I asked my eldest brother what this mysterious word meant. The word was "God"! The

state-imposed religion was atheism, which had its own dogmas and priests. The over-zealous crusaders for state-sponsored atheism did everything they could to eradicate any consciousness of God from the Soviet people. Their anti-God inquisition was unethical and merciless!

During a school lesson, the teacher asked us if anyone believed in God and if anyone prayed. She then announced that we were going to conduct an experiment. First, we would all repeat the prayer: "Oh God, please give us our daily bread." The whole class complied, and the teacher asked where the bread was. We were then told to offer a prayer to the late, great Soviet leader Josef Stalin: "Oh father Stalin, please give us some sweets." As we prayed, a roof tile opened and someone showered sweets on us as we sat at our desks. The experiment was over, and the teacher declared that although God didn't answer prayer, Stalin did.

I was puzzled but not convinced by this exercise in atheistic indoctrination. I thought for myself and rebelled against the system in my own way by not wearing the compulsory red neck scarf of the Communist Youth Pioneer movement. I was often caught by the teachers and told to put it on. They were not happy with me and threatened to tell my mother but actually, she was proud of me!

That Man!
One day, a woman on the bus gave my mother an illustrated children's book. Knowing that I loved drawing, she took it home, unaware that it was an illustrated children's gospel story. If she had known, she would not have accepted it.

Just as I had never heard the word "God" until the age of twelve, or understood what the word meant, so too I'd never heard of this Jewish man who was born in Bethlehem. Yet, as I read of the revolutionary Jewish rabbi who grew up in Nazareth, I was captivated by his story and drawn into the powerful drama. Suddenly, I turned a page and was shocked and horrified by what I was reading: "They can't do that!" I exclaimed. I was gripped by the unexpected twists and turns of the narrative, and my heart was broken as I read of the lies told about him and the injustice that was his trial. His execution left me distraught and in tears. But nothing could have prepared me for what I was to read next as I mournfully turned the page. Tears of joy replaced tears of sorrow as I saw that Yeshua had risen from the dead. Who was this wonderful man? I went to my room, and not knowing how to pray or what to say, I recited the Lord's Prayer as my confession of faith in Yeshua as my Messiah. In Hebrew the Lord's Prayer is a very Jewish-sounding prayer.

The Mysterious Book from Krym
In his childhood, my father used to go to Krym, near the Black Sea, for his holidays. One year, an elderly Russian lady dressed all in black beckoned him over and gave him a book as a gift. This book sat on the shelf amongst the many Russian classics from Pushkin to Dostoevsky. As I grew up, I read through all these books until I got to this beautifully bound book with its strange sounding name. When I had first picked it up, at the age of eleven, I didn't even recognize the words as Russian. My brother told me that I wouldn't be able to understand a "spiritual book" without spiritual insight, but I thought he was kidding

me. However, as I read, I didn't understand anything and so returned the book to its home on the shelf. Five years later, after the revolution I had experienced reading the illustrated story of Yeshua, I picked up the mysterious book from Krym. This time things started to make sense. I realised that Yeshua was a real historical figure. If he was who he claimed to be, then the account of his life should be totally out of the ordinary.

You're Not Stupid

Each day after I got home from school, I would go to my room to read more of the Bible. After a few weeks, my mother wondered where I was all the time and what I was doing. When she found out that I now believed Yeshua to be the divine Messiah and Saviour of Israel, she thought I had gone crazy. She said to me: "Rita, you are a clever girl; you're not stupid; you don't need to believe in this." After a while, my mother realised I had not joined a cult or lost my mind. She accepted that I was following my mind, heart and conscience. My father, though not a believer, thinks that Yeshua was the greatest rabbi to have every graced this planet.

Man or God

Wanting to know more, I looked for a place where I could learn more about Yeshua. After visiting a few churches where they just sang songs all night, I found some people who seemed to study the Bible seriously. However, they turned out to be "Jehovah's Witnesses". When it became clear that they taught Yeshua was just a man and not also the divine Messiah, I left them. After all, if Yeshua was not both human and divine, what was the point of his death? He could have only died for his own sins and not mine!

Address in a Bible

Some time later, as my family prepared to make aliyah (immigration) to Israel, a person in our town gave my older brother a Bible. It was an ordinary Bible, but on the back page was the address of a congregation of Israeli Jewish people who also believed in Yeshua. It was these few "chance" lines in the back of a Bible that led me to a congregation of Messianic Jews in a town south of Tel Aviv. And it was there that my faith developed and matured, and where I also met my husband. We now live in England.

Persecuted, not Persecutor

Something dramatic happens to many "Western" Jewish people when they see the real Yeshua, when they are emotionally free from the stifling prejudice created by the misconception that they have suffered as a result of actions done "in his name". However, like most Jewish people in the former Soviet Union, my experience of Christians was as the persecuted, not persecutor. After decades of Stalinist and Soviet oppression of the Jewish people in the name of atheistic Communism, many had no knowledge of Yeshua. He was not the cause of our troubles. Initially, in my case, he seemed to be just another persecuted Jew. I soon realised, though, that he was much more than that; more than the Stalinists, the Jehovah's Witnesses and the rabbis in Israel were ever willing to admit.

All about Eve

Eve

I was in Portugal but it wasn't sunny! I'd been robbed, I'd had an accident and my visa was about to run out. I was completely high, out of my mind on drugs, and I'd missed my plane – twice! Now I just wanted to get out of there.

"Listen guys, this is all the money I have. Just give me the plane ticket you have right now, wherever it's to."

They said, "Okay. England".

I said, "Fine".

I didn't want to go to England, but I was past caring.

Spiritual Journey

I was nearing the end of a long journey that had taken me to many parts of the world; a journey that began when, as a thirteen year old, I started to notice that there was something missing in my life! Surely you don't just go to school, go home, do your homework and play. I came from a very secular Israeli home, but I began to look for some spiritual input to my life. I looked at some of the fanatical Orthodox Jews who walked around the neighbourhood, but they didn't seem spiritual, just kind of scary. So I bought an expensive book about Transcendental Meditation, and I remember thinking: Why does it cost so much money to get to happiness? I examined many different cults, and got involved in Tarot reading and New Age teaching, but I was always looking for God. Yet I always found that what people taught me was a big lie. Everyone wanted something from me. Either they wanted my money, to take advantage of me or to brainwash me. I knew the Bible was real, but in Israel it was taught me from a secular point of view. So my life was really turbulent.

I had great grades in school, but that didn't interest me, so I left school. I then worked as a sales person and made a great score, but that didn't interest me either. I always had friends around me, and we went to parties and had a good time, but that didn't interest me, so I found new friends (I changed all my friends every six months!). It was as if I had everything, but I didn't want anything that I had. I had all the compliments, but I didn't care for them. At some point, I knew I had to leave Israel. I felt I was just dying. I started to travel the world, and it was in Japan that I came to an end of myself.

Insect Worship

In Japan, most people seemed to be in pursuit of money all the time. I made big money there but threw it all away gambling and partying. One day I thought, "Okay, let's check out Shinto". I sat down under a lovely tree beside a colourful temple in a beautiful garden, watched the monks walking real slow and listened as they banged a gong. I went to meditate because I had been so shocked by all the materialism I had seen. Suddenly something hit me from behind, and I realised it was a big insect. The trees were full of these insects, and as I looked at them, I noticed a sign declaring that the shrine was dedicated to that insect. I said to myself, "How low can you get! How can you worship an insect?"

From that point, my life started to go downhill, but I had a drug addiction and didn't care where I was going. I didn't even want to hold on to the thought that maybe I would one day find God. I went back to Israel, but I didn't find myself there. I wanted to go to Africa, but I couldn't get there. Finally, I went to Portugal and started selling oil paintings. I didn't care about money and didn't care about myself. If there was no chance of communicating with God, I didn't see any point in living.

But then one day I came to England. I started selling oil paintings, moving from apartment to apartment and going from job to job. I was really reaching the end. I had decided that this world had nothing to offer me. I had money, I had fun, I had men, I went to lots of parties, I travelled, but it was boring.

Salesman and Salvation

I decided I was going to kill myself, but I was in Leeds living next door to an English guy with an Israeli wife, she didn't believe in God but he was a "Yeshua freak" who told me about Yeshua. That really lit my fuse: "Yeah, you're going to tell me that God came down from the skies and did this and that!" As I was deciding about the way I was going to kill myself, I told him to bring his "Messianic rabbi" to me. I wanted to listen to him before I killed myself, because I had a suspicion that there might be a hell, and I didn't want to go there. So I met this guy. He looked like a salesman to me, and I thought he might have some sales tricks up his sleeve, so I said, "What do you want to tell me? What's your claim? What is your cult into?"

I soon realised that he didn't want to take advantage of me in any way. "Okay," I said, "Why have you come to this crazy conclusion that God can die?" He opened a Hebrew Bible – the Bible that I knew from school – and verse by verse he showed me that the Messiah would be born of a woman and would suffer and die. That very day I accepted Yeshua and decided not to kill myself! When I went home, I was on cloud nine. I started to read the New Testament. It took me four months, and I had many difficult questions: Why was Judas such a bad guy? Could I be another Judas? Could I make one mistake too many? What if I had the Holy Spirit and I blasphemed – would I be doomed? I was really struggling with the huge idea, that God himself – the infinite – came into a body to die for me – the nobody. He really loved me and I was not a nice person. He forgives me! It's difficult to comprehend!

But I knew I had found reality for the first time in my life. I went back to Israel thinking that people would persecute me when I spoke of Yeshua, but it didn't happen. Instead, a series of miracles happened. I found a huge congregation of Messianic Jews in Eilat, and I started telling people in the desert about Yeshua. I talked to people about God, and they actually listened to me, listened to the Holy Spirit speaking through me. I saw two other people come to know Yeshua as their Messiah during one month! I also sent my brother to the congregation in Eilat and, thank God, the superstitious occult influences are slowly being washed away from him.

I came to England from Portugal by "mistake" – but God knew what he was doing!

Light from the Tanakh

Tony

I was born to Jewish parents in Manchester and attended Jewish schools where, from an early age, I learned about God. One of the things I was taught was that he was omnipresent (present everywhere). When Jonah thought he could escape from God, he found it was impossible. The Psalmist declared, "If I go up to the heavens, you are there" (Ps. 139:8). I, too, sensed God's presence everywhere I went, but I was not taught about a holy God who hated sin.

Mitzvah or Messiah?
My family used to celebrate all the festivals, such as Passover and the Day of Atonement. We went along with all the traditions, but I did not see God as someone who could say through the prophet Isaiah, "...these people come near to me with their mouth and honour

me with their lips, but their hearts are far from me. Their worship of me is made up only of rules taught by men." (Isa. 29:13). Why did David say in Psalm 23:6, "I will dwell in the house of the LORD forever"? I once asked my father what happens to us after death, and he told me that we all go to heaven. This satisfied my curiosity about life after death, but in my Jewish schools I was never confronted with the text, "but your iniquities have separated you from your God; your sins have hidden his face from you." (Isa. 59:2). I had never been told that all my righteous acts were "...as filthy rags" (Isa. 64:6) or that "there is no-one who does not sin" (2 Chron. 6:36). I was lost and did not know God's forgiveness.

God said that without the shedding of blood there is no forgiveness: "It is the blood that makes atonement for one's life." (Lev. 17:11). But it contradicts God's Word to substitute atonement with *mitzvot* (good works), such as giving to charity and saying prayers. Even on the great Day of Atonement (Yom Kippur), following the destruction of the Second Temple, a tradition developed of offering special prayers that were said to equal sacrifices. Little did I realise that none of my good works could ever measure up to God's requirements for atonement.

Prejudice and Providence
During my youth I had an ingrained contempt for all non-Jews, whom I believed to be Christians, but this attitude got me in trouble when at the age of eighteen I went to work for a month on a kibbutz (communal village) in Israel. On the kibbutz, I met a Christian named Terry, whom I mockingly nicknamed "John the Baptist", something he did not appreciate. Terry complained

to the director, who reprimanded me for it. I complied, but my attitude did not change. Providentially, God had arranged for my room-mate at the kibbutz to be a Jewish man who believed Yeshua was the Messiah. For some reason he never spoke to me about his faith during my first stay in Israel, but God was to use him later.

After a few months in England, I returned to Israel to live on another kibbutz. There I met a Jewish girl I had known in Manchester who told me that there was a Christian on the kibbutz whose name was Charlie. She told me to be careful because he might try to convert me. "Not me", I said, "I'm not interested." But God had other plans. It turned out that my room-mate had a terrible problem with snoring and agreed to move out. While I looked for volunteers to change rooms with him, my former room-mate from the first kibbutz came to visit! This time, when I found out he was a believer I introduced him to Charlie, and God used this acquaintance to move Charlie into my room.

I Don't Want to Know

Charlie and I started discussing the Scriptures together, though I had not yet read any of the Bible apart from the book of Esther. Charlie did not tell me about Yeshua, until one day he referred to a chapter of the Bible that read:

> My God, my God, why have you forsaken me? ... I am poured out like water, and all my bones are out of joint. My heart has turned to wax; it has melted away within me... My strength is dried up like a potsherd, and my tongue sticks to the roof of my mouth; you lay me in the dust of death.... they have pierced my hands and my feet ... all who go down to the dust will kneel before

him – those who cannot keep themselves alive... They will proclaim his righteousness to a people yet unborn – for he has done it.

"I'm Jewish", I said, "I don't want to know about Yeshua!"

I had a big shock when I found out that the passage was not from the New Testament at all but was written by King David in Psalm 22, a thousand years before Yeshua was born! These and other prophecies, such as Zechariah 12:10, Isaiah 53 and Isaiah 7:14, eventually led me to believe that Yeshua was the Messiah.

I was so excited about these discoveries that in my exuberance I went around the streets telling everybody. I also went to see a Rabbi from the Hasidic Lubavitch group in Kfar Habad, a totally Orthodox village near the airport. I wanted to discuss Daniel 9:24-27, which records that the Messiah would die before the Second Temple was destroyed. This Rabbi told me that King Agrippa had fulfilled this prophecy. His answers, taken from a commentary, were so absurd that I was even more convinced that Yeshua was the Messiah. James, another believer at the kibbutz, who often took me to Messianic meetings in Haifa, asked me one day about who I thought Yeshua was. My answer was emphatic: "The Son of God, the Messiah of Israel!"

On that day, 24th December 1982, at the age of eighteen, I found peace with the God of my people – the God of Abraham, Isaac and Jacob – through our promised and long awaited Messiah. I was spiritually born from above. I repented of my sins and trusted Yeshua the Messiah as my Saviour. Now I can say like David, "I will dwell in the house of the Lᴏʀᴅ forever" (Ps. 23:6). My prayer today is that others will also make the great discovery that Yeshua is not just for the Gentiles; he is in fact the promised Messiah of Israel. If he isn't for us, of all people, how can he possibly be for them?

An Everlasting Love

Joseph

I was brought up in a Jewish family in Harrogate, England, and attended the local Orthodox synagogue with my family on Yom Kippur, Rosh HaShanah and the main festival days. I also attended cheder on Sundays for several years, learning to read Hebrew and finding out about the festivals in the Jewish calendar. I enjoyed the youth activities in Habonim, a Jewish youth organisation, and at the age of thirteen I had my Bar Mitzvah.

During the period of the Holocaust, my father had spent a year in two concentration camps: Dachau and Buchenwald. He was one of the last to get out alive in 1938, after which he came to Britain as a refugee. My family owned a photographic business in Harrogate and was well known in the Jewish community. I helped in the family business and studied at the Leeds College of Technology.

Round the World

At the age of twenty-two, I wanted to find out what life was all about. I was seeking reality, meaning and purpose, so I decided to travel around the world, beginning in Vancouver, Canada.

God evidently had his hand upon my life, and I met a young man from Northern Ireland who invited me to a youth group that met in a Baptist church on Sunday nights. It was there that I first heard about having a personal relationship with Yeshua the Messiah. I had no idea what "a personal relationship with Yeshua" was, but I received an invitation to attend a student life meeting at the University of British Columbia to hear a young man called Josh McDowell.

Josh McDowell surprised me by speaking quite authoritatively about how prophecy in the Tanakh had been fulfilled to the very letter in the coming of Yeshua the Messiah. As he was talking about the Jewish Scriptures, I was quite amazed to hear these facts and was willing to attend a second presentation a week later on how prophecy was to be fulfilled at the second coming of Yeshua. At a third meeting, Josh presented the evidence for and against the resurrection of Yeshua. Although his arguments were logical, I was very sceptical at the time; neither could I see what possible relevance the message might have for us today, nearly two thousand years later.

Revolutionaries for a Good World

Although I wasn't yet a believer, I was given the opportunity at a meeting to attend a leadership training institute, San Bernardino in Southern California. We were challenged first with the need for "a cleansed life". As a Jew, confession of sin to God was no problem for me because we did it every year on Yom Kippur. But then came the challenge to become "revolutionaries to help change this world for good", but the revolution had to begin in my own heart.

Amazingly, I stood up at that meeting, acknowledging that I was willing to allow God into my life and to receive Yeshua the Messiah into my heart as my Lord and Saviour. I didn't understand very much at that point but I was ready to give God a chance to work in my life. I thought that if this was real it would stand the test of time. Indeed, it truly has! I now know that God is real, that Yeshua is real and that God moves in mysterious ways in people's lives. My faith in Yeshua as my Messiah and Lord grew as I read the Bible, particularly the New Testament. And through passages in the Tanakh, such as Isaiah 53, I had come to the profound realisation and knowledge that Yeshua truly is our Messiah. He had proclaimed, "I am the Way the Truth and the Life, no man comes to the Father except through me", and I knew I had found the truth about what life was all about. It was centred in my personal relationship with Almighty God – the God of Abraham, Isaac and Jacob – through Yeshua the Messiah. I began to realise that what really mattered in life was having a right relationship with him and a knowledge of his everlasting love for me.

During my time in Canada, and subsequently in America, my faith in Yeshua as Messiah continued to grow. I established a photographic department at the headquarters of what is now called Agape and, while there, I caught a vision of what God was doing internationally. It was a very exciting time for me. After two years, I returned to Harrogate in England to help my father and mother in the family photographic business. It was the last place on earth I wanted to go to, but I was obedient to what I believed God wanted me to do.

Back to Shul

During my time at home, I attended our local synagogue on Shabbat. One of the elders was very concerned for me and spoke to my father. The elder offered to arrange for me to be accepted for training in the very Orthodox Jewish College associated with the Yeshiva in Gateshead in order to bring me back into the Jewish fold. My father agreed to this, and I received a telephone call inviting me to see the rabbi in charge of that college. I duly went the same day, and he invited me to stay. I was there approximately three weeks; it was a very challenging experience, which tested my faith in Yeshua. I learned about how the students studied Gemarah and heard about the disciplined life of prayer and study. Then I returned to help in the family business, helping to run the photographic studio.

With obedience comes blessing, and one day I introduced a young lady to my father and, surprisingly, he declared, "You are going to marry my son." Wow, how bold! And how miraculous, because that unlikely "prophetic word" came to pass!

Ruth Irene was a nurse, and we were married in 1975. Even though she was not Jewish, she was made welcome by many in the Jewish community. We have known God's rich blessing upon our lives together, having now celebrated our thirtieth wedding anniversary. We have two children in their twenties, a son who is studying medicine, and a daughter who is currently in Australia.

Ruth has often reminded me of my mother's last words to her a week before she died: "Oh Ruthy, how I pray to be like Yeshua." Being a Holocaust survivor, my father had suffered terrible persecutions for being a Jew, but when he became ill with cancer he testified how the Lord had spoken to him in the hospital saying, "You are safe; you are mine." He sincerely believed that it was Yeshua speaking to him.

Life is an exciting adventure as Ruth and I daily follow Yeshua, our Lord and Saviour. I have travelled to the Philippine Islands and seen God's mysterious, miraculous power at work there, and have visited congregations in mainland China, Hong Kong, Thailand, Sarawak and East Malaysia and have seen their steadfastness for the Lord. I have also seen God at work in many lives in Indonesia, and I know more than ever that he is real.

I still marvel that God's mercy and grace has been poured out on me and my family. It was only after many years that I discovered the secret of how it all began to happen. When I was at secondary school, another pupil asked two elderly ladies to pray for me. I believe it was because of their prayers that God's grace and mercy were shown to me. I still don't know who those ladies were, but one day we shall meet in eternity with great rejoicing!

Hear, O Israel

Debbie

I was brought up in an Orthodox Jewish home with my two sisters and brother. Although my family has ancestors from a variety of countries, including Poland and Italy, both sides have been resident in the United Kingdom for several generations. My sisters and brother and I went to Shul every Shabbat and to Cheder on Sunday mornings and midweek. I had my Bat Mitzvah along with three friends at a joint service one Shabbat afternoon. I was very secure in my Jewish identity and always knew and loved God. I socialised with many friends I had met through college and work, and one of them I married.

In and Out
My parents were horrified that I was "marrying out" and chose not to attend the wedding, so my only family at the

wedding was my older sister who was already married herself. I didn't see the rest of my family until just before my daughter was born in 1986.

My husband had been brought up in a Catholic family, but we lived a secular lifestyle. Our son was born in 1988 and my family organised his brit (circumcision ceremony) for us. I was delighted because even though I didn't keep a kosher home or attend shul anymore, my children were Jewish and it was important to me that my son should have his brit.

A Random Decision!

The story of how I came to believe Yeshua is my Messiah is really very simple. Well, simple in one way, but very complicated in another – a straightforward set of circumstances, but an inner struggle! Even when I knew in my heart that Yeshua is the promised Messiah of Israel, I struggled with the thoughts and feelings that "I can't believe in him because I'm Jewish."

All I really knew about Yeshua (or Jesus as I knew his name then) was that he was not for the Jews! Along with all Jewish people I could remember painful times of anti-Semitism, and even being held personally responsible for Yeshua's crucifixion! This accusation has been levelled personally at too many Jewish people, and experiences such as these are major stumbling blocks to Jewish people even considering that Yeshua might possibly be the Messiah promised by our prophets in the Tanakh. In my case, a boy came up to me as I was in school, walking into the playground with the other children and said to me "You killed Christ!" This is a traumatic accusation for any child to be faced with, especially a Jewish child who didn't even know the Easter story! Consequently, I'm always very careful how I talk about the Easter story!

Since being a child I had prayed alone every day, quietly saying the Shema and talking to God, and I believe that in His grace and mercy the Lord decided that the time was right to reveal the truth to me.

One Saturday afternoon in February 1991, as I was walking with my children past a church near where we lived, I noticed a sign outside that said, "Crèche (child-care) Facilities. Families Welcome". I decided to go the next morning. Why? I couldn't tell you, other than knowing now that God's hand was on my life, leading me in a certain direction. I wasn't consciously "searching" for anything, nor did I feel anything was missing in my life.

On my arrival at the church, I was greeted warmly at the door and shown where the children's groups were. I found myself in a lovely friendly atmosphere, and it was nice to see familiar faces; the lady teaching the Sunday school class was a neighbour who I used to say hello to in the street, and one of the children's schoolteachers was also there. The children felt very at home and enjoyed being in their groups.

Meanwhile, the service started, and after a time of worship the children went out to their groups. I sat back to listen to the sermon, and who did the preacher start talking about? Abraham! I thought, "Well, I know Abraham!" Although the worship time was quite foreign to me, Abraham was very, very familiar. The God of Abraham, Isaac and Jacob was indeed very close to me at this time! People spoke to me after the service, making me feel very welcome, and I decided to go back the next week. My husband had not joined us that morning, as he was working, but he started coming in the following weeks, shifts allowing.

We started attending this church regularly, and I knew without doubt that what was going on (i.e. the worship and teaching) was definitely "right", but I didn't understand exactly what it was.

Prior to this I had heard some basic teachings about Jesus, as anyone living in England has. My view was that people had to invent a 'man' to worship because they couldn't comprehend the magnificence and wonder of the God we Jews knew! I feel ashamed to have said that now, of course! But that was how I felt. I think God saw my heart, as he sees all our hearts and knows all our thoughts and feelings, and graciously led me to a place where the truth would be revealed to me. I believe that God guided me to walk into the church that particular Sunday. It was his way, his timing and with the people he chose. But I realised I still wasn't understanding the point.

What's a nice Jewish girl doing here?
Then Easter Sunday came, and I wondered what a Jewish girl like me was doing thinking of going to a church on Easter Sunday. I realised that I either had to stop going to church or find out what it was really all about. Although a part of me wanted to go to the service, another part was troubled, so my husband took the children on his own.

I had been attending regularly since February, and the pastor of the church had chatted to me, given me his card and said I was welcome to talk to him anytime. I knew the time had come, so I rang him. I was extremely nervous making that call! I remember how the answer phone came on, and I was so pleased just to be able to leave a brief message rather than go into a deep conversation. I think I knew that in doing so I was going a bit deeper than just dipping my toe in the water, as I had been up to that point. The pastor returned my call, and we subsequently met and talked; he suggested I read the Gospels. When we met again I had a whole list of questions for him! However, the questions were all minor points – I was convinced without reservation that Yeshua was the Messiah. I repented of my sin and asked Yeshua to be my Saviour and Lord.

Simple and easy? In one respect yes, because I was completely convinced that Yeshua was the Messiah, but, on the other hand, I went through torment thinking that I shouldn't believe this because I was Jewish. What surprises me still is that even at that time I was unaware of the significance of my being Jewish and the revelation of Yeshua being the fulfilment of everything my upbringing and faith had pointed towards. However, as I said a prayer of commitment, I thought I was the only Jewish person in the world ever to have done so!

Several weeks later, a friend of mine heard about a music group comprised of Messianic Jews who were playing nearby. She took me along (not without some significant obstacles arising to stop me going!), and it was there that I realised I wasn't the only Jewish person ever to believe in Yeshua! What joy! You really *can* be Jewish and believe in Yeshua. Gradually, the whole picture unfolded, as I realised how every part of my upbringing had led me to this place. I now understand how the Jewish festivals are connected to Yeshua, and, in studying the Tanakh and the New Covenant, I can see how the Messianic prophecies and promises accurately point to Yeshua HaMashiach.

Headhunters and Revolution

James

I grew up in an Orthodox Jewish home in a predominantly Jewish area of North London. Both my parents were doctors, and my brother, sister and I had a happy, busy and trauma-free childhood. My paternal grandparents – the Abromovitches – had come over to England from Russia to escape the pogroms and settled in the East End. Similarly, my maternal grandparents – the Steins – avoided Nazi persecution by moving from Poland in the middle 1930s.

As a child, I knew much about the Tanakh and God from my Jewish school and synagogue. My parents, and to some degree their families, had made it through the Holocaust, and our Jewish identity was important and emphasised. I knew nothing of the claims of Yeshua until much later in my life, because we had been told to stay away from Christians and not to speak "that name", as "he" was one of many who falsely claimed to be the Messiah.

Manila

Whilst still in my teens – barely out of school – I was involved in jointly managing a catering company; then I studied at Sussex University, obtaining a degree in Sociology in 1986. Through a chain of coincidences, I decided to accept a position as Community Development Director in the Philippine Government, carrying out community initiated projects sponsored by the Asian Development Bank in Manila.

Looking back, I can see the decision was crazy! I was leaving the work I knew and going to a country I had never visited before, to do work of which I had little experience in a language I couldn't speak!

I arrived in Manila in 1986 at the height of the anti-Marcos revolution. Everything was new to me, but I quickly grew to love the people and my work in the Department of Urban Poor. I was working among prostitutes, street children and squatters and had offices and a house in Boni Avenue near the Municipio. After three years I felt very much at home. I had contact only with Filipinos, which was fine, but soon God was going to bring me into contact with someone whose simple story would bring very unexpected results in my life.

Headhunters

I had always had a strange curiosity about the Philippine headhunting tribes, and eventually I agreed to manage an irrigation project in the Sierra mountain area with a group known as the Ilongot people. I lived with them for some months and learned their story. They told me that they were "of the trees" – the literal meaning of the word Ilongot – and explained that they took people's heads only because they were afraid of anyone who came into their village. In an amazing story of God's grace, the people had been protected until Filipino missionaries shared a message that affected them so much that their lives were completely changed. I could see the change – it was undeniable – these were not "religious" people or hypocrites, but straightforward people who sincerely saw the truth.

Later, when I returned to Manila, I organised some meetings for my department in the hope that other projects could be started. I also contacted a number of people in missionary organisations that had first-hand experience in these areas. I asked them to come and tell us about different people groups, in order for us to be better prepared for any projects we might carry out. Somehow, at the time, it did not register with me that they were all *Christian* missions, as my prejudice at that time would not have allowed me to have had any contact with them!

Not your Bible!

An American missionary, Jay – a soft spoken, gentle family man – who had been in Ilongot country himself, asked if I would be interested in having Bible studies with him. "No", I replied, "not in *your* Bible!"

"We can study your Bible then", he quickly replied.

I agreed, as I relished the thought of contact with some non-Asians for a change, and in my pride thought there might be a thing or two I could show Jay!

Our studies took place on a weekly basis in Jay's home. We studied the Tanakh from Genesis and Exodus, and every week he would leave me with some questions. By the next week I had the answers and wanted to move on.

I had known the Bible stories from my childhood, but I now saw them in a new way. I saw clearly that God of the Bible was a personal God and that he was interested in the lives of each individual: Abraham, Isaac, Jacob, and Joseph. I could also see that God was supremely holy. These clear and simple truths led me to the automatic realisation that I was certainly *not* holy!

The Challenge of my Bible

By the time Jay and I reached Leviticus, I was beginning to be convicted of my need of something more. One week, Jay posed a question that stirred my heart: "What makes you think that you no longer need blood sacrifices?" Well, as a Jew, I knew the logical answer – there had been no temple since 70 CE, so there was no longer any need for sacrifices; forgiveness was now obtained through prayer, "Jewishness" and Yom Kippur.

However, during that whole week, as I searched for the answer to Jay's question, I realised that the Jewish answer with which I had been raised was *not* in my Bible! What *was* the answer then? I couldn't work, I couldn't sleep or eat much; I read frantically my Tanakh from cover to cover at least three times that week, but I could not find any answer other than the one that seemed clear: sacrifices were the *only* biblical way to obtain forgiveness of sins.

Revolution

I know this is hard for many Christians to understand,

but I was so convicted about the need for animal sacrifices that I imagined Jay and his family must have been offering up burnt offerings to be right with God. The next week, I sat on the edge of Jay's couch and told him about my fruitless search. He explained that there was an answer but that it was to be found in the New Testament. I did not want to even let him read it to me. The New Testament, I objected, was only for Christians.

Jay replied that the New Testament was written by Jews and was addressed mainly to Jews.

I wasn't sure.

"Does it *really* answer my question about sacrifice?" I asked.

"Yes".

"How much do I have to read?"

"One verse!"

I took some convincing but eventually I agreed, as I had to know the answer. Jay said he wanted to read to me what the last Jewish prophet said when he saw the Messiah: "Look, *the Lamb of God*, who takes away the sin of the world!" (John 1:29)

As I heard those words, I suddenly understood the sacrifice God had made; it was like a light bulb had been turned on. I saw clearly for the first time why I had been raised believing there would be two Messiahs: Messiah ben David who would reign as king and Messiah ben Joseph who would suffer and die. Messiah would indeed reign, but first he had to sacrifice himself.

That single verse was the only New Testament text I needed at that time. In my relief and delight, I told Jay that I understood why Abraham had been willing to sacrifice his only son and why God had replaced Isaac with a ram. I understood why God had clothed Adam and Eve with animal skins after their sin in the Garden of Eden.

Now I understand why every year at Pesach we remember the lamb and the blood that caused the Angel of Death to pass over the Israelite houses, and why we break the Afikomen, which stands for "the one who is to come".* Now I can understand the mysterious verses concerning Messiah's sufferings in chapters 52 and 53 of Isaiah, and many verses in the Psalms and elsewhere.

I stayed on in the Philippines and helped a little in community development until I left in 1989. Then I returned to the United Kingdom, moving to the USA in 1991. I met my wife-to-be, Kimberly, in Oregon, and we came back to the UK in 1994, when I became Dean and Teacher at a Bible College. After completing a sabbatical year in 2003, I finished my studies with a PhD in Philosophy and Religion, and we returned to the USA. We have three children, and I am so glad to be able to teach them their rich Jewish ancestry and the possibility for them too to know, love and interact with God just as Abraham, Isaac, Jacob and Joseph did.

---

* Editor's note: Some scholars, including the highly respected Jewish writer David Daube, point out that the tradition of breaking the Afikomen, the second of the three pieces of matzah at the Passover Seder, dates back to before the time of Jesus. In his monumental study, *He Who is Coming*, Daube showed that the Greek word *afikomenos*, from which the term Afikomen is derived, means "the coming one". In the days of Jesus, messianic expectation was high because Rome was the fourth kingdom foreseen by the prophet Daniel, in whose days the Messiah would come. According to Daube and others, when Jesus broke the Afikomen at the Last Supper and said "This is my body", he was claiming to be "the coming one", the Messiah.

Marie and Sheila Hyams were both successful, sophisticated business women. But, beneath the veneer, all was not well. Both had a great spiritual hunger and a fascination with Yeshua.

The Most Important Day of My Life

Marie

My parents were Jewish, and my earliest memories of childhood were quite happy. We lived in North East London and although mother and father did not follow their faith strictly, we observed the festivals because, I was told, it was tradition! I sometimes went with my parents to the synagogue, but the service didn't really mean much to me. I couldn't understand what was going on, because I had never learned Hebrew, and no one explained to me what was happening. We didn't speak about God at home, and though I had heard that God made the world, to me he was very remote, somewhere "up there".

I was seven or eight years old when I first heard about Yeshua in religious education classes at school. I was fascinated by him. He seemed to be very special, telling wonderful stories and curing people with terrible diseases. I vividly remember running home after one lesson to tell my mother all about the lesson, only to be told very firmly, "We don't talk about *him*! We are Jewish." I couldn't understand why, if Yeshua was a Jew as I had been told, I couldn't talk about him. And why had he been killed? Why was my mother annoyed with me for talking about him?

There must be something more...
In adulthood, when I met with friends, we would often talk about the meaning of life: Why are we here? Where are we going? Everyone was of the same opinion – make the most of life because when you're dead, you're dead, and that's it! Some of these people were well educated and intellectual; they thought I was rather naive to believe "all that religious stuff". But if they were right, I couldn't see the point of it all. There had to be something more.

For most of my life I worked as a secretary in the City of London. There are some lovely churches in the Square Mile, and I used to spend many lunch hours visiting them. St. Paul's Cathedral was close at hand, and I went there many times, not to study the architecture, beautiful though it is, but to look in fascination at William Holman Hunt's painting, *The Light of the World*, portraying Yeshua standing at the door of the human heart. A friend at work was to be married in church, and when I asked whether she believed in God, she said she had never really thought about the matter. But she did think it was a pity that I was Jewish because Yeshua came into the world for the Gentiles!

Born again?

In 1993, the year started badly for me. My health was not good, there were problems at home and I was at a very low ebb. Then, in early March, a childhood friend whom I had not seen for a long time came to see me. She had become a Christian and was full of joy. I had heard of people being "born again", though at that time I didn't know what the term meant.

She gave me a book, *What Christians Believe*, which I read two or three times. We began to see each other more frequently, and each time we met she brought more books. I eventually began to read the Bible and discovered that Scriptures I had become familiar with through Handel's *Messiah* – "For unto us a child is born", "He was despised and rejected", "With his stripes we are healed" and many more – were from the Tanakh! I had always assumed that, because they were about Yeshua, they were from the New Testament.

All is revealed.

When I started to read the New Testament, everything became clear. I began to understand the mystery of Yeshua's death: He came into the world to fulfil the Old Testament prophecies; his sufferings and sacrifice were for the sins of his people.

The most important day of my life was 21st May 1993, the day I asked Yeshua to come into my life. A verse from John's Gospel (6:37) was going round and round in my head all day: "All that the Father gives me will come to me, and whoever comes to me I will never drive away." That evening, all the discussion, all the reading, went from my head to my heart. God had sent his Son into the world to save me. After many tears, I asked Yeshua to come into my life, to forgive my sins and to renew me. I was so sorry to have kept him waiting outside the door of my heart for so long. But when I opened the door, he entered my life.

It's a Wonderful Life

Sheila

I have always loved Yeshua. I was taught about him at English Infant School I attended and loved everything I heard. When I was older, I learned that he had been crucified and that they'd placed a crown of thorns on his head. I could not believe it. How could this be!

Marie and I used to talk and talk about him. If there was a novel about Yeshua, we had to read it. If there was a film about him, we had to see it. We were so excited about the TV series *Jesus of Nazareth* in the mid-seventies, and we watched every episode. We had a great hunger to know about Yeshua, although we never read the Gospels – or the Old Testament for that matter. What was the point? "They" (our family and the religious leaders) told us that Yeshua was "not for us" – but why not?

No Yeshua; No God!

There were no answers, and so all these thoughts were pushed to one side, although from time to time they would come to the surface. I totally turned away from God. Yeshua said, "No one comes to the Father except through me" and, though I had never read those words before, that was what I felt in my heart – No Yeshua; no God!

I lived a secular life, and since the majority of my friends, especially the very intellectual ones, appeared to manage very well without God, it seemed all right for me – most of the time.

However, during times of disappointment, especially bereavement, I needed and longed for spiritual comfort. When my darling mother died and my world collapsed around me, a particularly close friend gave me the best advice she could muster: she told me to join a tennis club or the Conservative club! That, she confidently predicted, would help me to "get out and get over it"!

Freedom

When the Lord sent Marie's friend Joan to us with many books about Yeshua, I couldn't stop reading. It seemed at last that all my questions were being answered. During that time, my godson was baptized. Naturally, I attended the service and from that time my eyes began to open and my ears began to hear. I began to meet real Christians; I saw and heard them worship God with sincerity and joy, and their kindness and love towards me was overwhelming.

At first there was some resistance, some inner conflict. But after meeting and talking to some Jewish people who believed in Yeshua, I knew without doubt that it was right for me to ask Yeshua into my life. The feeling of guilt was over – buried for good – and my life began to change completely. I felt free. I could forgive those who had hurt me, and the bitterness I felt towards them began to disappear.

Wonderful!

In part one of my working life, when I was a fashion designer going to the Paris Collections and so on, people would say, "How wonderful! How exciting!" In part two of my working life, when I was involved in selling the most luxurious and expensive properties in London and organising luncheons and parties for the glamorous and wealthy, they would say, "How wonderful! How exciting!" Wonderful! Exciting! It is my life now that is really wonderful and exciting. Learning about Yeshua – that's wonderful, that's exciting! Reading God's Word – that's wonderful and exciting! To live without Yeshua the Messiah is to have an empty and unfulfilled life. I thank God that after all these years I know the truth – I, Sheila Hyams, born to Jewish parents, can at last worship my Messiah, my Yeshua and have the inner peace for which I had always longed.

God in an Unexpected Place

Rosamund

I grew up in South-East London, and my family was from a Reform Jewish background. I did not think much about religion but had Hebrew lessons on a Sunday and enjoyed attending synagogue with my father on Friday nights. I had few encounters with the Christian faith.

I went to a Church of England boarding school for eighteen months when I was eleven. We had to go to chapel twice on a Sunday, but I can't remember hearing the gospel, the good news that Yeshua's death and resurrection could save us from the punishment due to us for our sins. Instead, we would sing some Psalms and listen to dull sermons which did not have much to do with the Bible. A typical talk would be about Francis of Assisi and how he loved animals! For many years this coloured my view of Christianity as being dull, grey, insipid and irrelevant.

At Religious Education lessons in my next school in Bromley, Kent, we learnt how Yeshua commended people's faith in his ability to heal them. I used to think that if I had been around at that time, I would have had the faith to believe he would have healed me. However, I still generally regarded the Christian faith as boring, except for church weddings with the lovely solemn vows – wonderful – I wanted that! Also, I thought that missionaries who left home to go to places like Africa were really brave. My sixth form English teacher showed us poetry that spoke of the Christian teaching that Yeshua would return to the earth. I was astounded at how these "grey" people could have such a daring belief!

After A-levels, I was due to go straight to university, but I found the prospect stifling. At the time, I had begun to seek God and was reading books on Buddhism and Hinduism. However, it was all too complicated, and I thought that God should be simple to find. I pretty much ignored books on Christianity as I still considered it boring!

I then spent eight months on a kibbutz (communal village) in Israel, learning some Hebrew, working and meeting fellow Jewish young people from Morocco, the USA, Germany, France and Iraq – as well as more Orthodox Jews who seemed to take their faith very seriously. I returned to Britain in the summer of 1976 and decided to look for God in the faith into which I had been born. I even postponed my first day at Nottingham University to go to synagogue on Yom Kippur, the most holy day of the Jewish year. For the first time in my life, I was seriously observing Yom Kippur by fasting and praying. However, I found myself disappointed to find that people were more interested in how others were coping with the fast, than looking for God. Leaving synagogue I felt disappointed that, for all my efforts, I still did not know the Lord. If he was not to be found on the day when sins are atoned for, when could he be found? Nevertheless, whilst at university I continued to be observant. I arranged with my personal tutor to be released from Saturday morning tutorials so that I could keep Shabbat; I joined the Jewish Society and regularly visited the Shakespeare Street synagogue.

Cut Inside

When I arrived a day late at the halls of residence, I was intrigued to discover that my neighbour was confident that she knew God, so I asked her what she believed. I was totally unprepared for what she told me. She explained that I would one day have to stand trial before God and give an account of my life. I felt as though I had been cut deep inside, because I knew there were things in my life that were not acceptable to a holy God.

The other thing that surprised me was how well she knew the Bible. She knew far more about the Tanakh than I did, so I became determined to study it for myself. I was struck when I read Isaiah 29:13:"These people draw near with their mouths and honour me with their lips, but have removed their hearts far from me". This was exactly what I had felt!

But more surprising were the verses that agreed with what I had learned from my neighbour whom, I discovered, was a born again Christian. I saw that sin was part of our human condition:"For there is not a just man on earth who does good and does not sin" (Ecc. 7:20).

The Truth Dawns

I learned that God himself would do something to cleanse us from sin: "In that day a fountain shall be opened for the house of David and for the inhabitants of Jerusalem, for sin and for uncleanness." (Zech. 13:1)

From the book of Isaiah, I saw that the Messiah would bring us peace by taking the punishment for our sins: "But He was wounded for our transgressions, He was bruised for our iniquities; the chastisement for our peace was upon Him, and by His stripes we are healed." (Isa. 53:5)

The prophet Micah even revealed where the Messiah would be born: "But you, Bethlehem Ephrathah, though you are little among the thousands of Judah, yet out of you shall come forth to Me the One to be Ruler in Israel, whose goings forth are from of old, from everlasting." (Micah 5:2)

A New Covenant

Through Jeremiah I learned that God was going to make a new covenant with the Jewish people, even greater than the one established through Moses: "'Behold, the days are coming,' says the LORD, 'when I will make a new covenant with the house of Israel and with the house of Judah ... I will put My law in their minds, and write it on their hearts; and I will be their God, and they shall be My people. No more shall every man teach his neighbour, and every man his brother, saying, "Know the LORD," for they all shall know Me, from the least of them to the greatest of them', says the LORD" (Jer. 31:31-34).

More Than Conviction

Only when I was sure that Yeshua was the Messiah promised in the Jewish Bible did I open the New Testament. As I opened Matthew's Gospel and read, "The book of the genealogy of Jesus Christ, the Son of David, the Son of Abraham..." I realised that this was no Gentile book; this was meant for the Jewish people. Reading beyond the opening verses, the words and teachings of Yeshua impressed themselves on me as the truth.

Some weeks later, I came to the point where I knew that Yeshua was the Messiah, that he had died for my sins, was buried and rose from the grave on the third day. But it had to be more than just an intellectual conviction; I prayed and asked him to forgive me and come into my life. My life was completely changed. I had found what I had previously searched for in vain. The words of Yeshua were true: "I am the way, the truth, and the life. No one comes to the Father except through Me." (John 14:6)

After university and Law College, I began working as a solicitor in London. There I met another Jewish believer in Yeshua who was to become my husband. Robert and I eventually married and a couple of years afterwards I left work to start raising a family. We now have three sons and still live in London.

Twice Chosen

Peter

In 1938 my mother, then twelve years old, was living in Kiel, Germany, with her parents and ten-year-old sister. One night a rampaging mob descended on our family home, intent on causing as much destruction as possible to the property and possibly the people within it. Fortunately, our family was in rented accommodation, and the owner was present. On being informed that the property and furniture were owned by Germans, the mob moved on to find other "Jews".

This was obviously a terrifying experience for my mother's entire family, so they went into hiding in an uncle's loft in Hamburg where they believed they would be safer. Needless to say, it wasn't long before they were raided, rounded up and sent off to the camps. However, my grandfather had a certificate to accompany the Iron Cross he had won in the service of the German nation at the Somme. On producing these items, his family was spared and the soldiers moved on to the next Jewish home. Clearly the family was going through desperate and traumatic times. At that time England was willing to receive Jewish children but not adults so, in December 1938, my grandparents made the courageous decision to put their two daughters into the hands of who-knows-who and send them to an unknown future in a foreign country. The sea crossing to England took place in a force ten gale! In due course my mother settled into her new country, married a non-Jewish Englishman and had three children, of whom I am the youngest.

Emotional Wall

I was born in 1958. My recollections of family life feature many incidents of stress, conflict, and disharmony, with the odd smattering of domestic violence. For the most part, my parents lived separate lives in the same house, my father having his own room.

The legacy of this unhappy situation was three insecure and emotionally battered children. My older brother was sent to boarding school at the age of eleven, as my parents could no longer cope with his behaviour. I dealt with the situation by building a wall around myself. At school I would never show pain or emotion, and problems there were resolved by physical violence rather than discussion. Although this gained me a form of respect from peers and the nickname "Tank", I was left feeling more isolated and lonely than ever.

In times of desperation I prayed to God and, to my astonishment, my prayers were answered. I was utterly convinced of the reality of God although, at that time,

I was not consciously aware that I was descended from Abraham and was, therefore, Jewish. There was no religious activity at home.

Fresh Start

My chance to show God that I could change and repay some of his goodness to me came when I was eleven years old. I was sent to a large secondary school in the East End of London with only one other child from my primary school! This was my big chance; a fresh start, a new life, decent people for friends and no more violence, swearing or fighting. It worked for about three weeks! I made new friends who weren't hooligans – although they weren't goodie-goodie creeps either – and I kept out of trouble.

I was a big lad for my age, which had always worked to my advantage. Now, suddenly, my size was a problem. To be big and non-violent was like hanging a big neon sign around your neck inviting anyone who fancied their chances to pick a fight. If this was God testing me, then I failed him miserably. Once I began to fight back, my new friends were horrified while the scumbags I had been trying to avoid wanted to be my "mates". I was back to square one and feeling more miserable and depressed than ever.

Looking for Something, Finding Something Else

Eighteen months later, I decided I needed female company. The only place I knew I could find it was the church youth club that my sister attended. So, with strictly dishonourable intentions, I went along! What an eye opener that was, in every sense! I met thirty-five young people who were slightly older than me, the majority of whom were keen young Christians who were neither wimps nor geeks, just people who were very keen to tell me about, and show me, the love of Messiah. They loved the Word of God, prayer and singing. We went rambling, ice skating and rowing, met in each other's homes and had loads of good times. But Yeshua and his love were always at the centre of things.

At the club itself, we usually had a twenty-minute devotional time at which God's Word was taught in a clear and relevant way. At last I understood that the God who had graciously answered my prayers over the years had actually done so much more for me than I could have ever imagined. I knew that thousands of years ago a good man, maybe even a prophet, had died on a cross, but I hadn't seen that the crucifixion had any connection or relevance to me. Now I realised that God had sacrificed his Son precisely because I could never put things right with him by myself. All the accumulated garbage and filth of my life could never be cleared or washed away by me. Only someone pure and holy could pay the price for my sin and give me a new start with God by dying in my place.

God sees the big picture. I needed to be humbled and brought low before I could respond to his love and the calling of the Holy Spirit. With his strength and enabling I could be different, born again, a new creation! I asked the Lord to forgive me for all my past sins and to help me change and to be Lord of my life.

My life certainly changed big time! I now felt loved and secure in the Lord. I had the help and support of some great godly people who were teaching me. There would be many tough times and challenges still to come, but I had found a peace and joy in the Lord that I had not known before.

When I applied for baptism, I was told to wait and reapply after twelve months! I wasn't angry or resentful and reapplied a year later and was finally able to go through the waters of baptism, in obedience to my Lord. When looking back at my time with this Bible-teaching church, my greatest sadness is that they taught "replacement theology". Replacement theology is the idea that the Jews were once God's chosen people but they blew it by rejecting Yeshua and were replaced by the Christian Church. And I never questioned it!

Now I see that if God were to reject the Jewish people, he would be breaking his covenant with Abraham! Throughout the last two thousand years, there have always been Jewish people who have followed Yeshua. After all, the original Church and Yeshua himself were Jewish!

For many years, I didn't give much thought to my Jewish roots. However, when meeting Jewish people on my travels overseas, I was very touched to be so warmly greeted, wished "Shalom" and urged to make aliyah. On one occasion, whilst walking down Leather Lane in London, I met some Jewish people who also believed in Yeshua the Messiah! I was absolutely chuffed. I had never heard of "Messianic Jews" before! To my shame, it wasn't until years later that I tracked down a Messianic Fellowship with whom I could meet on Erev Shabbat. What a joy to meet with children of God's covenant with Abraham, who are also God's elect from his New Covenant. God does not break his promises. That includes his promises to Abraham. Twice chosen – what a privilege!

The Glass is Full!

Estelle

For as long as I can remember, I have thought that Yeshua was the promised Messiah, but because I'm Jewish I felt I shouldn't think like that. On one occasion when I was quite small I was in shul and I said, "If you're waiting for the Messiah you'll have a long wait. He's already been." It was not a good idea; the only thing it got me was a clip round the ear! So for many years I kept my conviction well hidden. However, in January 1997, I made a phone call that changed my life forever.

It had been a really bad year for me in 1996; my marriage had failed and my life felt as if it had suddenly fallen apart. I felt isolated and alone. My oldest and dearest friend came to see me. Hilary, like me, was born and brought up in Liverpool, and we'd been friends since we were ten years old. Although Hilary now lives in Eastbourne, we've always kept in touch through the years, and see each other at least a couple of times a year.

Despite that, when Hilary told me she'd become a Christian, I wasn't impressed. I had no idea what Hilary was talking about because, as she wasn't Jewish, I assumed she was a Christian automatically. It would take me a long time to realise there was a difference between someone saying, "I'm a Christian" and actually being a Christian. My friend told me that Yeshua could help me. I'd been brought up to believe that we had our God, and the Goyim had their God. I thought that Jews believed in one God and the Goyim believed in three gods.

We Don't Pray Like That

Hilary went back to Eastbourne and told her friend Margaret about me. Although Margaret didn't know me, she very kindly sent a letter telling me about herself and her journey of faith. She gave the name and phone number of someone who could help me, but it was up to me to phone her. For days I read and re-read Margaret's letter, and eventually I plucked up the courage to make the call. It was Saturday 7th January 1997, and I was ringing someone I didn't know and had never met. Yet it really was a phone call that would change my life. I spoke to a lovely lady called Elizabeth who told me there were other Jewish people who believed in Yeshua and that I wasn't alone. We spoke for hours, and I felt as if we'd been friends for years. Elizabeth told me about the British Messianic Jewish Alliance and said that I would still be Jewish if I believed in Yeshua. I felt so reassured when I heard that. Nobody had ever told me this before. I remember when Elizabeth first came to my house and gave me a card with the Lord's Prayer on it. She asked if I would pray aloud what was written on the card. I found this very hard, as I'd never prayed out loud before. I said I was Jewish and that we didn't pray like that. I'd never prayed for myself; my rabbi had always prayed for me!

The Goyim Hate Us

Elizabeth introduced me to a lady who ran a Bible study on Friday mornings. I asked what I needed to take to this study group and was told that a Bible would be a good idea! I'm an only child and was brought up in an Orthodox Jewish home. My mother kept kosher, we went to shul every week, and we kept Shabbat and all the festivals. I'd never even seen a Bible with both Old and New Testaments in the same book. Some friends bought me a complete Bible, but just in case I was being conned, I read my own Jewish Bible first. My own Tanakh was as new as when I had received it for my Bat Chayil when I was thirteen years old. When I finally read the Bible I'd been given, to my surprise the Old Testament was the same as my own Tanakh! But when I read the New Testament, the words came alive. I was reading about Yeshua, the promised Jewish Messiah; it was fantastic! I had my eyes opened, and things would never be the same again. I was forty-five years old, and I felt I'd been robbed all my life because I'd been brought up to believe that Yeshua was not for me. Bible study was one thing, I thought, but there was no way I'd go into a church. I was afraid that if I went, God would strike me dead.

The lady who ran the Bible study asked if I would like to go to hear a Messianic believer called Michele Guinness. "What's a Messianic believer?" I asked. "It's alright," I was told, "Michele's Jewish, like you". I discovered that Michele would be speaking at a Christian Fellowship, but I didn't know what that was either. The reply came that it was a church that didn't look like a church; it had ordinary chairs instead of pews! I decided to go, and we walked into a room full of people, at the back of which was an Israeli flag. I thought that was very odd. What was a flag of Israel doing in a Gentile church?

Both my parents were Jewish, as are all my family. My mother's family have been in Liverpool for over 100 years, but my father was a Polish Jew who came to England at the end of World War II after all his family had been killed in the Holocaust. When I was about five years old, my father told me, "Always be careful, *meine kinder* [my child], the Goyim hate us. Sooner or later they'll stab you in the back". Because of the persecution we have experienced at the hands of Gentiles through the ages, many Jews, including me, have had a deep-seated fear of non-Jews. We fear that history will repeat itself and that once more we'll find ourselves having to pack up and move on.

How Did I Get Here?

I enjoyed listening to Michele Guinness that evening, and felt that she was talking directly to me. This was the first time I had listened to someone who was Jewish and also believed in Yeshua; all the next week I kept thinking about what I had heard. The next Sunday morning I went for a walk, leaving everyone else at home in bed. I had no idea where I was going, but I mysteriously found myself outside the Christian Fellowship, of all places. I looked at the notice board, which announced that the Sunday morning service was at 10.30. I looked at my watch – it was 10.15 – and I heard music coming from inside the building. The next thing I knew I was inside; I still have no idea how I got there, but as I stood at the back of the room not knowing what to do, the pastor came over and introduced himself. I just blurted out that my name was Estelle, and I was Jewish. I was asked to stay where I was while the pastor went to find his wife. Then a lady came and introduced herself. Suddenly, this person I had never met before flung her arms around my neck and said that the church had been praying for me.

Praying for me! How could anyone pray for me when they'd never even met me? I found out much later that the fellowship had prayed for a long time for Jewish people. From that first morning, I knew I'd found somewhere I belonged. I'd never felt like this sitting in the ladies gallery in shul. I have two children, Brian and Debby, both born and brought up Jewish and, after a few weeks Brian asked if he could go to the fellowship with me. My husband Peter, who is a Gentile, later became a believer in Yeshua.

Family or Faith

Although both my parents died some years ago, as an only child I have enjoyed having a large extended family of aunts, uncles and cousins. However, I kept my faith a secret from my family because I knew in my heart what their reaction would be if they found out I believed in Yeshua. One Sunday morning, I got home from the fellowship and found my daughter Debby in floods of tears. One of my aunts had phoned while I was out, and Debby had told her I was at church. I called my aunt, who was furious. How could she face the Jewish community knowing what I'd done? I was given a choice. I could have the family or I could have Yeshua, but I couldn't have both. I was trembling from head to foot but the Lord gave me the strength to say, "If that's the choice, then I choose Yeshua."

My aunt cursed me, wished me dead and that was that.

A Family Never Known
I was asked to speak at my fellowship on National Holocaust Day on 27th January and found it really hard to do. I wasn't speaking about six million strangers, but about my own family: the grandmother I was named after but never had a chance to meet; the aunts, uncles and cousins I had never known. My family I had now didn't want to know me; they thought I was a traitor to my own people. But after my talk about the Holocaust I felt the need to know more about my background. I found out about my grandparents Max and Jane Cohen, but I didn't even know my grandmother's maiden name or when she had died; I only knew that my grandparents had come separately from Russia to Liverpool and had then met and married. As I had so little information about my family, when I made enquiries, I was told it was highly unlikely that I would get very far in my search.

Families Reunited
Some time later I was once again asked to do a presentation about the Holocaust. I really didn't want to do it, but Peter said, "Estelle, you have to do it; if you don't, who will?" This time I got the young people from church to help me. I wanted to show that anti-Semitism did not originate with Adolf Hitler, but my head seemed

to spin as I thought about the family I never knew, and the family that didn't want to know me because of my faith in Yeshua.

A couple of weeks after my Holocaust presentation, I received a phone call from the Jewish Archives in Liverpool to say that someone else was looking for information about my family, and that my grandmother's maiden name was Smolonski. I was asked if it would be in order to give my phone number to a lady who turned out to be my cousin's daughter. I hadn't seen her since she was a child, but now she was a grown woman with children of her own. She very kindly sent me a copy of our family tree, but I was upset to discover that my uncle had died and that I hadn't even been informed. I asked her to remember me to her mum, my cousin Edna; to my surprise, Edna wrote to me! Even after many years, I recognised her handwriting. Edna said she would understand if I didn't reply to her letter, but I did, and through her I found out who had died, who had married and who had had children. I also learned that the aunt who had been angry with me for following Yeshua was eighty-three and in poor health. My aunt never apologised to anyone, and I believed she would never contact me again, but I let my cousin know that if our aunt ever wanted to see me I would visit her.

One evening, as we were having a meal together in the kitchen, the phone rang and Peter answered it. He called me: "It's your aunt's voice!" This was the first call I had received from her in eight years. "Estelle", she said, "Will you come to see me?" I replied that of course I would, and we arranged that I would go to see her that Friday afternoon.

I told Peter that I'd go on my own as it would not be an easy visit. When I arrived, I rang the bell. My uncle opened the door and gave me a hug. Then my aunt hugged me so tightly that I thought she'd never let me go. She apologised for her harsh words and I explained that I couldn't live my life the way she wanted me to live it.

"Yes, I know," she replied.

Later, I had the courage to send my testimony of how I came to believe in Yeshua to my cousin. My family may not yet understand my love for Yeshua, but they at least accept that I have the right to believe as I do. I feel so richly blessed having Yeshua in my life. He's not just a part of my life; Yeshua *is* my life, He is my reason for living.

A long time ago I was asked, "Estelle, is the glass half full or half empty?" For years that glass was half empty, but now it's overflowing.

That Unspeakable Name

Barry

I grew up in a modern, academic Liberal Jewish family in North London. I was the son of two shrinks, a psychoanalyst and a psychotherapist – what a mix! Hard work and Woody Allen were the two major driving forces in my childhood!

At the age of thirteen, I had a lovely Bar Mitzvah and then got involved with ULPSNYC, the Liberal Jewish Youth network. My family always kept Shabbat with the Friday night Kiddush prayers as well as celebrating all the other Jewish festivals. I went to Israel many times and spent a year there after university. My family went to synagogue regularly, but although it was lovely and friendly, I never developed a personal relationship with God. I thought the Bible was interesting but antiquated and believed that most of it had little relevance to modern life.

Talking to Thin Air

I had many Jewish friends and hoped to marry a nice Jewish girl one day. Then, at teacher training college, I fell in love with a nice Christian girl! She had a strong faith in this "Jesus", and I used to tease her: "What do you mean, you talk to Jesus? You're just talking to thin air!" Inwardly, however, I was jealous of her faith.

We got married, and then we found out that she couldn't have children. It devastated us both. I became an angry, frustrated husband because I realised for the first time that I was not fully in control of my life. If there was a God, a real God, he had stopped me from having children. I wanted to find him and find out what was going on. It was a crisis, and I was desperate.

My wife and I had talked about adopting children; this had led us into debates on how to raise the children. She felt so strongly that they must be told that Jesus (Yeshua) is the Messiah. I argued that they could be brought up both Jewish and Christian. She wouldn't budge – she would have to tell them the "truth": Jesus is the Son of God. There was no compromise.

I was angry. It seemed that any adopted children we might have would be "Christian". That was a shock to me. I had always wanted and believed that my children would be Jewish. I decided to cautiously investigate a bit more about this "Christianity"... for the sake of the children.

Not That Name

I went to a church nearby, and I felt real love in the place! The people really loved Yeshua. I wanted to join in with them, so I sung the lovely hymns – but I couldn't bring myself to say the Gentile name of Yeshua. Being Jewish,

I believed that it was wrong even to speak his name, so when we sang songs like *It's all about you, Jesus*, I just stopped singing when we came to the name of Jesus. At the end of the service, I was invited to find out more about Yeshua by doing an Alpha course. No strings attached. I thought, "OK... for the sake of the children..."

So I did an Alpha course and found it a great way to express all the cynicism I had grown up with. As a young person, I had been told that the explanation of the resurrection was that "Yeshua's dead body was stolen by his disciples." I was also told that Paul had made up the New Testament, turning Yeshua into a God. I was even firmly told that Paul was not actually Jewish! I know now that these were lies that have been told to the Jewish people by our leaders in order to immunise us and to protect us from "converting".

Then I found out what I consider is the biggest lie of them all: "You leave the Jewish people if you believe in Jesus". This horrendous lie has kept Jewish people in fear of Yeshua and genuine Christians for 2000 years! This is, however, understandable when you think how so-called "Christians" have treated the Jewish people – my people – throughout history: The Romans (after Constantine), the Spanish Inquisition, the Crusaders, the Czars and even some of the Church during the Holocaust. Many Christians that I have met today are ashamed and truly sorry for the persecution of Jews by 'Christians' in the past. Many "Christians" have forcibly converted Jews in the past, and this explains our inherent fear of Christianity. But then I heard Helen Shapiro (perhaps the most famous Messianic Jew in Britain) explaining that Jewish people become Messianic Jews, not Gentiles, when they accept Yeshua – our Jewish Messiah!

Being a Messianic Jew is an affirmation that there is nothing wrong with being Jewish and when it comes to Yeshua it is not an "either/or" situation, it is both/and. You don't leave the Jewish people at all; in fact, I became more completely Jewish than I had before! I was overwhelmed with joy and relief when I heard this! I gave my life to Yeshua and stepped into freedom. Immediately there was a special peace in my heart and soul. I felt that I had found the truth I had longed for. I felt that I had found God and that there was hope. I had never expected Yeshua to be the Messiah – but he is! I was able to cry out much of the pain in my life to God.

My parents weren't so happy.
After three months, I had plucked up the courage to tell them. I phoned them to tell them I had something important to say. I drove to their house and went straight past to the nearest coffee shop. Finally, I sat down with them, shaking, and said: "I have become a Messianic Jew..." At first they responded, "Is that it? We thought it was something really serious!" Then they said, "Well, it could have been worse – you could have been on drugs!" Finally, they concluded, "What's a Messianic Jew? You can't be Jewish and Christian! You must be meshuggeh! (crazy)" I reassured them that I was still Jewish... and I am still reassuring them years later (at least they accept now that it wasn't just 'a phase'!) At the same time – but just before me – my sister also became a Jewish believer in Yeshua. I'm afraid my parents had to cope with a "double-whammy"!

Through the Valley of the Shadow

Since that time, Yeshua has helped me through hard times: divorce, singleness, changes of location and jobs. Through my own pain, God helped me develop compassion for others, and I have been able to minister to people in need. God led me to India to minister to street children and children with AIDS.

Throughout my time as a believer in Yeshua as the Messiah of Israel and hope of the whole world, I have sought to develop my Messianic Jewish identity. I have enjoyed fellowship and spiritual growth in several Messianic fellowships and churches. I have danced and acted with the New Jerusalem Dancers, and I am now a Religious Education teacher and an amateur actor living in London. God has led me through difficult times. In the pain following my divorce, I sought comfort and refuge in the Psalms, and this led me to write an adaptation of the life of King David for the stage. With the help a Messianic Fellowship in Ilford, the play was performed at a local theatre. A Jewish man who came to see it was very moved, and soon after he too came to the conclusion that Yeshua is indeed our Messiah!

Another turning point in my life occurred in Israel when, as a Messianic Jew, I prayed with a Palestinian born-again Christian. I had grown up learning to fear and mistrust Arabs, but now I am convinced that the only hope for real, lasting peace between Arabs and Jews is what Yeshua HaMashiach can do for our fractured relationships.

My life has come full circle, and God has crowned my painful experiences with joy as I am now married to Alison, a wonderful Messianic Jewish woman.

My Sweet Lord

Deborah

"My Sweet Lord" is the title of a song written by the late George Harrison of The Beatles. It praises *his* Lord, Krishna, a mythical figure deified in Hinduism.

Growing up, I was a Beatles fan, and when I reached my early twenties, being somewhat stressed out, I reacted positively to media advertisements for a relaxation technique called Transcendental Meditation. After all, it had been The Beatles who had embraced this spiritual discipline and commended it to my generation. And if The Beatles were for it, it must be okay!

A Non-religious Religion?
TM (as it became known) was brought to the West from India by a friendly guru named Maharishi Mahesh Yogi. It was advertised persuasively as non-religious, even non-spiritual, certainly not Hindu, and therefore no threat to

or contradiction of the Western mindset, be that Christian or post-Christian. It promised great things to all enquirers, and at relatively little cost in terms of time or finances. I came from a secular Jewish background and had been spiritually curious all my life. Still, it wasn't spirituality I was expecting from Transcendental Meditation so much as a way to lose weight and to stop smoking!

After a few introductory talks, I was invited to a TM teacher's nice suburban house. The students had been asked to bring along a white handkerchief and a piece of fruit as an expression of gratitude. At that time, I had no idea that this expression of gratitude was in reality a votive offering to a Hindu deity.

That day, after the final introductory talk, I was invited to accompany the TM instructor into an adjoining living-room and to kneel next to him in front of a portrait of an Indian figure. The teacher then began to say something, but, as he was using an Indian language, I didn't know what he was saying. Had I known that my initiator was praying in Sanskrit to the figure above me, I wouldn't have minded, because at that time all religions were much the same to me; back in those days I was wandering through the spiritual marketplace.

The teacher whispered a word into my ear, telling me that this word was the "mantra", a sound without meaning that I should repeat silently in my mind. The sound would soon "disappear" and translate into a sublimely peaceful state of mind, namely transcendental meditation. The technique was so simple that a child could learn it; it was merely the repetition of a meaningless sound. There was no complex or esoteric technique to be acquired. Transcendental Meditation was true meditation, we were told, removed from religious tradition and available to everyone.

Having been instructed in Transcendental Meditation, I went home that day feeling no different than before. But, for the next fifteen years, I meditated twice a day as I had been taught, once in the morning and once in the evening. The routine was to find a quiet place, sit in a normal way (not cross-legged like a yogi), close one's eyes and silently repeat that meaningless mantra. The sound would then disappear from the mind, leaving just a pleasant state of relaxation, the only unusual aspect of which was that time seemed to speed by extremely quickly, so it often seemed that almost as soon as one had started meditating, the twenty minutes had passed.

I never did regard TM as a spiritual exercise, but accepted the organisation's line that this technique – at least on the basic level to which I had been taught – was designed not to give busy people spiritual enlightenment but rather relaxation and a new mental freedom from the stresses of everyday life. It sounded not only harmless but also very attractive. For a while, that's how it seemed, and since I wasn't interested in deriving anything spiritual from TM, I continued on my spiritual journey.

Five years later, my spiritual journey took an unusual turn (especially for a Jewish TM practitioner!); for I accepted that I was a sinner in need of the salvation that only Yeshua the Messiah could give, and I gave my life to him.

I still had a lot of questions. I knew that Yeshua was Jewish, yet it seemed strange that it was mostly non-Jewish people who worshipped him. I had experienced anti-Semitism from some people who claimed to worship a Jew! However, even with most of my questions unanswered, I still knew that I needed Yeshua.

"The anguish of the grave came upon me."
I don't remember exactly when TM began to be a problem to me. It may have been through my exposure to the Bible. It may have been because my experience of meditation began to change from positive to negative. Certainly these two factors began to express themselves slowly but insistently.

There was another factor in operation too, and that was denial. Anyone who has learned TM is pretty much left alone, they are not solicited for money or required to join an organisation. So it was possible for me to meditate and not feel part of a body or subscribe to anything. I was aware that TM was derived from Hinduism. However, I believed – because they told me and because I wanted to believe – that it was possible to use meditation divorced from Hinduism, in much the same way that people imagine yoga (a Sanskrit word meaning "yoke" or "union") can be simply a form of physical exercise.

The seemingly unobtrusive TM organisation was arranged into local groups, and occasionally I went to informal meetings, which included a meal and listening to taped teaching from the Maharishi. I would ignore or privately deride any attention the group gave to this. Occasionally one heard of esoteric experiences that were available to the advanced meditator, but I was uninterested in advanced meditation techniques; I just wanted the basic technique with no spiritual strings attached. I was, of course, in denial, and this was the nature of the denial – that one could meditate on the basic level and be untouched by its Hindu roots. But TM was becoming less a choice I made every day and more a necessity. I had never gone in for the Hindu element so, I told myself, TM was just a physical and mental relaxation technique; it had nothing to do with spirituality. I didn't want to learn advanced techniques, so I told myself I was okay.

The trouble was that I was not okay. Where TM had once been an option, it was now becoming a necessity; if I didn't meditate morning or evening, I would experience unpleasant sensations and could recover only through meditation. The feelings were similar to feelings of stress – a feeling of tightness, almost like a vice around my head accompanied by mental confusion – but different in that they couldn't be relieved by exercise or rest, but only by going into the meditative state.

The other change was that the duration of the meditation was increasing, as I would lose track of time sometimes for over an hour.

The obvious answer was to stop practising TM, but whenever I tried to go without meditating, the mental discomfort was such that I had to start again. I asked the local TM group for an explanation. They told me that the unpleasant mental sensations were simply the symptoms of stress that people who didn't meditate experienced routinely. Because TM relieved stress, these symptoms were only what I would have experienced if I hadn't learned how to meditate; so it followed that if I stopped practising TM, these unpleasant mental sensations would be with me all the time.

Certainly, it did feel much like stress when I didn't

meditate – a constriction around the head, mental confusion. Perhaps, after all, it was as the TM instructors had said, nothing more than mental tension. I remember visiting a friend who practised TM and I noticed that she also seemed very stressed and confused, and I began to wonder if there was more to this than met the eye.

For several years I remained caught in a trap. I wanted to stop practising this increasingly intrusive and compulsive technique, but couldn't.

"He told me everything I ever did."

In the summer of 1992, I participated in a residential week-long study course. Living for a week with other Christians, it felt particularly wretched being in bondage to meditation – a practice which was anathema to evangelical Christians but from which I was powerless to escape. One night, as I was falling asleep, I recalled the commandment, "You shall have no other gods before Me." I suddenly understood that through meditation I was effectively serving another god and, as I fell asleep, I wondered if God would forgive me.

The following afternoon was free, and I went for a walk, during which I happened to meet Howard, another course student. We stopped to chat, and then he did something rather unsettling. He said, "Can I ask you a question?" I said yes, and he asked if I really knew that God loved me. I answered in theological terms, but inside I was hurt and furious. Of course I understood the gospel! How dare this stranger ask me that? What did he mean? What did *he* know? I headed back to the college deciding to avoid him for the rest of the week.

By the next day, my feelings had changed from not

wanting to speak to Howard to wanting to talk to him. Strangely, during the day everyone else seemed to "disappear", leaving me alone with the strange stranger! Curiosity got the better of pride, and as we sat in the common-room area, I asked him why he had asked me if I really knew that God loved me. He said he had been praying for everyone on the course (at which point I had him pegged as a definite religious nutcase!). Howard then told me that when he had prayed for me, he had heard the Lord saying these words: "She thinks there's something I'll never forgive her for. But I know all about her. And I love her. And one day, I'm going to heal her."

Had this episode been portrayed on film, at this point the screen may have shown the room spinning! I also felt as though time had stood still. I remember thanking him, and then there seemed to be people around; the day returned to normal. The difference now was that I had been left with a promise from God, and I held on to that until the day he fulfilled it.

By that winter, the oppressive symptoms I had experienced through TM were worsening. I would try not to meditate, but I would feel as though a cord was tightening round my head so that I had to give in and start to recite my mantra. When I did meditate, it would be for increasingly long periods of time; I would seem to blank out or lose time, coming to after more than an hour but feeling like only a few minutes had passed.

I was feeling increasingly desperate and longed to be able to stop meditating. I hung on to the promise the Lord had made to me: *"She thinks there's something I'll never forgive her for. But I know all about her. And I love her. And one day, I'm going to heal her."*

I knew that day would come but wondered when, and I was concerned just how bad things would get before it came. I visited the central London TM centre, went through their standard meditation check, and asked the instructor why I had felt so bad when I tried to stop. He gave me the answer I'd heard years before, that these symptoms were merely the stress that people who don't meditate feel all the time. It wouldn't make sense to give up meditation.

"All things work together for good."
In 1993, I was working for a large Italian company and found that I wanted to import various Italian cultural features into my life. One such was a coffee percolator! Instant coffee was fine for me, but real, percolated coffee seemed especially nice, sophisticated and "Italian". I was given a percolator and so, the first thing each morning, I enthusiastically went through the routine of setting it up by putting a filter into place, spooning coffee in, and letting the water percolate through it. For about twenty minutes, the little machine percolated away in the kitchen, a most satisfying concept to someone who aspired to things Italian! I'll return to the coffeepot later ...

Around this time I had bought a book of stories written by people who had left occult practices, but, being still partially in denial, I didn't associate myself with them. Although the book included TM among the occult practices, I just thought the author didn't understand. At the back of the book was a list of organisations, so I phoned the Reachout Trust and spoke to a man called Derek. I told him I was desperate to stop TM but couldn't. I also explained that I hadn't learnt it with any interest in associating with Hinduism. Derek said that it was impossible to separate any practice from its roots.

That night I felt very bad. It had been wonderful talking to someone who understood. But it would be a long time – at least a month – before I could visit their office. That night I prayed to Yeshua for forgiveness and for help.

When I woke up the next morning, I began my normal routine. Since I had got the coffeepot, this routine had changed slightly. Meditation previously would have been my first action of the day. This was because until I had meditated, I would experience not just the normal fuzziness we sometimes feel on waking, but such mental confusion and oppression that normal activities would be quite difficult until I had performed the morning meditation session. But now I would hold off meditating just long enough to set up the percolator.

So I went into the kitchen to set it up. It took a few minutes, and in those few minutes I began to notice something rather odd. If I hadn't spent those few moments making the coffee, I wouldn't have had the time or space to notice the change, but would have launched directly on waking into meditation. But now, in the kitchen, I began to notice that something had changed. I didn't actually feel confused or oppressed any more. I was making the coffee quite easily. This was unusual and actually quite scary. I went back to bed, feeling rather strange. The compulsion to meditate still wasn't there. I felt something like fear. I didn't know what was happening. For the first morning in over ten years, I was experiencing absolutely no need to meditate. I wondered what was going on. I still felt no need to meditate. This was a workday and I would have to get ready soon. I got ready for work and drank a cup of percolated coffee, still not quite believing what was happening. The compulsion to meditate had completely disappeared. There was no longer a tight band around my head, disappearing only when I meditated. I had been freed from Transcendental Meditation!

"All are liars."

When I learnt TM, there was no Internet on which to check it out. Now TM has its own website, and an enquirer can access numerous testimonials both positive and negative. I read elsewhere that in the mid-seventies, thirty thousand Americans were learning TM[1] every month. TM had been brought into the school curriculum, into business training and the professions. It was practised and endorsed by clergy who had believed the lie that TM is unaligned with religion. However, a change came when the TM organisation was successfully sued in the American Federal Court on the charge that it was, in fact, Hinduism in disguise.

As a result, the TM organisation was compelled to publish the English version of the prayer recited in Sanskrit (the "puja"). The Indian figure before whom I had knelt and to whom my teacher had prayed years before was the Maharishi's dead teacher, Guru Dev, considered in Hinduism to be divinity manifested in human form. To quote a former TM instructor Vail Carruth:

> Thus the puja is intended to alter the consciousness of the … candidate in a way that opens the mind to

the influence of the "great Masters". Its function is understood to be the establishment of a spiritual ... bond between the new meditator ... and Maharishi and his Hindu tradition of Masters ... [2]

The translation into English from Sanskrit reveals lengthy devotions and prostrations to Hindu divinities. No wonder meditation had made me feel bad! Testimonies are now available of meditators who encountered demonic manifestations while meditating and suffered spiritual/mental breakdown. The mantra, far from being the "meaningless sound" that TM claims it is, is the name of a Hindu "god" that is actually a demon[3].

According to former Hindu priest Rabi R. Maharaj, who is now a disciple of Yeshua: "The mantra both invites the being to enter the one using it and also creates the passive state in the meditator to facilitate the fusion of beings."[4]

Vail Carruth reports: "I began to become aware of the presence of spirit beings sitting on either side of me when I was meditating. Sometimes at night, uninvited, they would sit on my bed. I thought they were my guardian angels. Once I looked at one of them, and I saw a small dark creature with sharp teeth, who looked more like it wanted to devour me than to bless me. I did not consider the possibility of Satan or his demons at the time ..."[5]

Such phenomena, commonly experienced by meditators, remain unexplained by the TM organisation. I discovered that I hadn't been alone in experiencing lapses of consciousness while meditating, times which I would be unable to recall later. Evidently this so-called "black-out phenomenon" is common in TM but remains unexplained.[6]

TM Today

Increasingly, our secular Western society has welcomed Hinduism and Buddhism and has incorporated them into the New Age spirituality accepted in business, education, and parts of the church. Indeed, TM no longer needs to hide its true spiritual colours. Today the Maharishi's Indian base at Rishikesh welcomes young people from all over the world. A high proportion of these are like me – Jewish – and many are young Israelis who include training in TM as part of their gap year after army service.

On the internet I found testimonies of meditators who had experienced unpleasant symptoms similar to my own. However, I found just as many who reported pleasant and affirming experiences. My own experiences started off pleasant, becoming oppressive only after a few years of meditating. These practitioners of TM may be having good experiences – for a while.

I feel then that it is inappropriate to argue against TM solely from the point of view of experience. I should emphasize that my literally overnight transition from being unable to stop meditating to being completely free of it was not explicable in terms of psychological positive-thinking techniques or wish-fulfilment. I repented of my involvement in TM, of believing a lie for many years, and I had prayed to Yeshua the Messiah. The next day I woke up unattached to TM. We are free only by turning to Messiah Yeshua as Saviour and Lord because, as the New Testament says, "The reason the Son of God appeared was to destroy the devil's work."[7]

Endnotes

1. David Haddon and Vail Hamilton: *TM Wants You!* (Baker Book House, Michigan, 1976), p.19

2. Ibid., p.46

3. 1 Corinthians 10:20

4. Rabi. R. Maharaj: *Death of A Guru:* Hodder & Stoughton, 1978, p. 219

5. David Haddon and Vail Hamilton: *TM Wants You!* (Baker Book House, Michigan 1976), p.67

6. Ibid., p.40

7. 1 John 3:8

Journey of Discovery

Yacov

Both my parents are Jewish, though neither were observant Jews. My mother grew up in an assimilated Jewish family in England, but I was born in South Africa. A couple of generations ago, my family chose to hide their Jewish identity, and many chose to attend Anglican churches rather than synagogues. This has been a common phenomenon in the Jewish world over the centuries as Jewish people, seeking to escape from anti-Semitism, have hidden their true identities. Thanks to my father's influence, however, I was circumcised as a Jewish boy on the eighth day.

Sadly, my parents seperated and divorced when I was very small. My mother brought me to England, where she married a Gentile when I was six. At no time did she or anyone else on her side of the family reveal my Jewish identity to me.

I grew up attending Anglican boarding schools, where I was required to attend chapel. I found chapel dull, and I remember on one occasion taking a book with me, intending to read it surreptitiously during the service.

Out There, but Not for Me

At the secondary school I attended, most boys would get "confirmed" between the ages of fourteen and seventeen. Many boys, including me, chose to get confirmed as a social ritual, rather than out of any genuine religious conviction.

I believed that there was a God out there somewhere, but my primary interests at that time were football, girls and drinking beer on Saturday nights! However, I studied hard during my A-level years as I was determined to win a place at Oxford University. At Oxford, one of the Christian Union leaders invited me to a CU meeting. I remember little of what the speaker said except that he had a personal relationship with Yeshua. Though I didn't understand what "a personal relationship with Yeshua" was, I was intrigued.

More Important than Football

Over the next few weeks, things began to fall into place. I realised that after the crucifixion, Yeshua did not remain dead; he rose from the grave and it was therefore possible to know him personally. I remember staying in my room one Saturday afternoon to read a book called *Basic Christianity* by John Stott. I had turned down the chance to watch a football match which, looking back, was a miracle in itself!

As Stott explained who Yeshua was, why he had died,

and what his resurrection from the dead meant, my understanding grew. Finally, Stott wrote about a choice that I needed to make. I could accept Yeshua as my Lord and follow him in a real way – not simply by paying lip service to him but by living my whole life in obedience to his commands. This would be difficult and costly as I might be misunderstood or even rejected by others. Alternatively, I could reject Yeshua, which would probably result in me having a much easier life. However, on 3rd February 1996, I prayed to God, asking him to forgive my rebellion, and I accepted Yeshua as my Saviour and Lord.

My life began to change. My religious exterior was replaced by a genuine desire to attend church weekly and hear the Bible explained. My previous vague belief in God was replaced by a personal relationship with him. This has not always meant an easy life, but at its best it has brought me great joy and a real peace. Initially my family was alarmed by the changes but, over the years, they have come to accept the genuine faith I have found.

Who am I?
I graduated from Oxford in 1999 and moved to London to study at Law School. Throughout my time at school, university and Law School, my Jewish identity remained hidden to me. I had one or two Jewish friends, who, noticing that I had a Jewish surname, asked if I was Jewish. I always denied it – out of genuine ignorance – but, looking back, I'm amazed that the penny didn't drop sooner!

In 2001, I moved to Birmingham to start work as a trainee solicitor. There, my Jewish identity finally began to catch up with me. A lady in the church I was attending noticed my surname, and she too asked if I was Jewish. What really swung it, though, was attending a cousin's wedding in 2002. At that wedding, I met many distant relatives, some for the first time. When I told one of them that I attended church and asked if he did the same, he looked at me rather shocked and said, "No, we're Jewish; as are you!" I didn't really know what to say in response! My great-aunt, whom I had not seen for many years, told me that one of her sons, Richard, was a Messianic Jew, who was teaching at a theological college. That intrigued me!

I made contact with my cousin Richard shortly afterwards, and for the first time, the family background and my own Jewish identity began to become clear to me. Consequently, I started to appreciate references to the Jewish people in the Bible in a new way. When the apostle Paul wrote of a "remnant" of Jewish people who believed that Yeshua was the Messiah, I realised that this remnant included me!

The time came when I needed to look for a new job. I wanted to stay in Birmingham, but the legal market in the city was flat at the time, so I was forced to look elsewhere. I secured a job in Leeds, where I moved in September 2003.

Navigating My Identity
Reading Paul Johnson's *A History of the Jews*, I was struck by the many examples of the way Jewish people had suffered at the hands of the Church over the centuries. Before I moved to Leeds, both Wendy and Richard told me about someone who ran a Messianic Fellowship

there. They explained that it was a meeting for "Messianic Jews", Jews who had accepted Yeshua as Messiah. I made contact, more out of curiosity than anything else, and started to attend the Messianic Fellowship in addition to my "regular" church. Initially the meetings seemed strange: songs and prayers in Hebrew and English, a sermon looking at an aspect of doctrine or a book of the Bible from a Jewish perspective, and "Kiddush" at the end of each meeting. "Kiddush" is a small meal of bread and wine with which Jewish people mark the start of the Sabbath every Friday evening. The leader of the group explained the rationale to me: the aim was to provide a setting where Jewish people who wished to, could come freely to hear about Yeshua in a comfortable, non-threatening environment, without feeling that they needed to discard their Jewish identity. Given what I was starting to learn about the history of the Church's treatment of the Jewish people, this made sense to me.

Part of the Ultimate Minority

As I continued to attend the Messianic Fellowship, the liturgy became more meaningful, and it was a joy to celebrate the Jewish festivals of Rosh HaShanah, Hanukkah, Purim, Succot and Pesach. I saw how these festivals pointed towards Yeshua, the Messiah. I read Stan Telchin's *Betrayed* and Graham Keith's *Hated without a Cause? A Survey of Anti-Semitism*, both of which impacted me deeply. I saw again how much the Jewish people have suffered at the hands of the Church over the centuries, and why it was so difficult for Jewish people to believe in Yeshua. At the same time, the books of Telchin and other Jewish believers in Yeshua confirmed my belief that Yeshua was nevertheless the Jewish Messiah! As the leader of the group explained, Messianic Jews were "the ultimate minority". Some unexpected correspondence with my father, who sent my Hebrew *bris* (circumcision) certificate to me, reinforced my growing awareness of my own Jewish identity and the realisation that I too was one of this "ultimate minority".

From early 2004, I started to identify myself as a "Messianic Jew". Some Christians were surprised; most were at least mildly interested. Some asked me questions about Israel and Judaism, but I had to disappoint them with my lack of knowledge! Thankfully, no one was openly hostile, though there were some misunderstandings. One man asked, "So you used to be Jewish?" Explaining the complicated background to my Jewish identity, I assured my questioner that I could be Jewish and also believe in Yeshua. The two things were no more incompatible than being English and believing in Yeshua! On another occasion, at a friend's house, a professing Christian suggested that one might expect to recognise Jews by their "big noses and bags of gold". The anti-Semitic stereotype stung. I was too stunned to respond!

I began to read the Christian press in a new light. As I discovered more of my own family background and the grim legacy of the Holocaust, book titles such as *Forgiving Hitler* made me distinctly uncomfortable. An email of concern to the publisher of that book was well received. On the other hand, some contributors to a certain Christian newspaper made consistently derogatory and, in my view, very unfair comments about the state of Israel. I realised that, in many ways, the Church remained an uncomfortable place for Jewish people. I began to write to the Christian press, challenging both anti-Semitism and its more subtle modern cousin, anti-Zionism.

In 2005, I had the opportunity to visit the German city in which some of my ancestors lived before they migrated to England. My family had at one stage been influential within that town, funding the synagogue and setting up a bank. Yet not all had managed to leave Germany, and to discover that some thirteen of my family had perished in the Holocaust was a sobering experience.

I consider myself 100% Jewish and 100% follower of Yeshua: a Messianic Jew, following in the footsteps of the apostles and the first followers of Yeshua. My family, mindful of the fate of some of our ancestors, has also raised eyebrows at the prospect of my "coming out" as a Jew. Yet the Jewish people retain a special place in God's plans (Rom. 11:25-26), and Yeshua is the Jewish Messiah: how could I deny either?

From New Age to New Life

Sarah

I grew up in a liberal Jewish family in Highgate, North London, where there was a lot of love. From the age of five I attended synagogue, which was where I first encountered God.

When I was a teenager, my parents divorced, which caused me a lot of pain and grief. I felt as though the foundations of my life had collapsed, and I began to search for peace and meaning to life. I began to take drugs and to study religions such as Orthodox Judaism, Buddhism, and New Age philosophies in an attempt to find answers to my questions. Instead, I found that those philosophies were empty. There was nothing to grasp.

Inner Peace
I felt I had tried everything, and nothing could help me. In 1980, my father had started a New Age business and,

being influenced by the New Age ideas, I started making ceramics for that market: palmistry hands, phrenology heads and Egyptian god figures.

The following year, while I was studying for a degree in Ceramics, my mother threw me out of the family home. It was a very painful time. I felt hopeless and tried to fill my life with things such as drink and drugs, but I wasn't satisfied. I went to counsellors and clairvoyants, but they couldn't help me. I went to Israel for two weeks and visited Bethlehem on Christmas Day. On my second visit to Israel in 1987, I visited a hostel in Jerusalem where they held services on Friday nights. There I heard about Yeshua, but I didn't think it was for me. So, I returned to England.

A year later I travelled to Egypt and Israel; I arrived in Eilat suffering from food poisoning after eating bread at a Bedouin camp. On the beach at Eilat, I met a girl called Naomi who seemed to have a deep inner peace, something that was lacking in my life. She explained that Yeshua was a Jew and that he was the God of Abraham, Isaac and Jacob, and that he came and suffered for Jews and Gentiles. She maintainted that it was important for me to identify with the Jewishness of Yeshua and not to lose my identity as a Jew.

Emotionally Paralysed

Naomi read a story from the fifth chapter of John's Gospel about Yeshua healing a paralysed man at the Pool of Bethesda in Jerusalem. Yeshua asked him, "Do you want to be helped?" I was feeling *emotionally* paralysed, and when I heard those words, it was as though God had spoken them to me by his Spirit.

I was quite resistant to Yeshua and felt I would be betraying Judaism if I believed in him. But after talking to many people who did believe in Yeshua, and asking many questions, I realised the gospel of Yeshua was all true, that God in his love had heard my cry and was reaching out to me. As Naomi spoke to me, I felt his compassion and conviction reaching out to me through her and saw a peace in her that I'd never known. I remember that day very clearly; I was lying down with my head in my hands quietly crying, realising that I was in the presence of a holy, loving God.

A Reason to Live

I also realised that I'd lived a life of self-indulgence and rebellion, separated from God. I realised Messiah had died for all the wrong things I'd done and that I could be forgiven. A few days later, in Israel, I asked Yeshua to come into my life.

I feel I have been given a reason to live and that life has a meaning. Yeshua has filled the void inside me with his peace, and I don't have to take drink or drugs to escape the pain. Not everything is perfect, but God has given me a hope for the future and assurance of eternal life.

After I realised that the pottery I was producing wasn't pleasing to God, I started to make Passover plates and Havdalah goblets. Eventually, I gave up the pottery business and trained to become an English teacher. I spent two years working as part of a ministry team in St. Petersburg, Russia, teaching English through the Bible.

The following verses from the Bible speak of what God has done in my life:

I waited patiently for the Lord; He turned to me and heard my cry. He lifted me out of the slimy pit, out of the mud and mire; He set my feet on a rock and gave me a firm place to stand. He put a new song in my mouth, a hymn of praise to our God. Many will see and fear and put their trust in the Lord (Ps. 40:1-3).

Not Ashamed

Joe

I'm a second generation Messianic Jew, which means that both my parents are Jewish and believe that Yeshua is the Messiah, and I happen to agree with them. Every year as I was growing up, we'd have a Passover meal with Hebrew songs and readings, so Jewishness and belief in Yeshua always went naturally hand-in-hand for me. My earliest memory is of my mother reciting the Aaronic blessing to me before I went to bed:

> May the Lord bless you and keep you;
> May the Lord make his face shine upon you and be gracious to you;
> May the Lord lift up the light of his countenance upon you
> And give you his peace.
> Amen.

Youth

When I was young, I had an illustrated children's Bible, and while I found Yeshua interesting (he seemed to like children more than other adults did), I was fascinated by the stories in the Tanakh. At the age of six or seven I decided to read the Bible from the beginning. I liked Genesis, because it included the story of Joseph, after whom I was named. From what I understood, he was the best of all his brothers and didn't mind letting them know it either. I found I had a lot in common with Joseph!

But what really interested me was the book of Joshua. That was where the Bible got really exciting; I'd waded through Leviticus, Numbers and Deuteronomy – knowing that it was still the word of God and that I had to give it my utmost attention – but Joshua was thrilling. The wars and battles are great to read when you're that age; Joshua is an action book, with the Canaanites as the bad guys and the Israelites as the good guys. From the accounts I read, it was so clear that God was on Israel's side. It was such an intricate and detailed historical account that from a young age I was convinced that it couldn't have been made up.

We were taught about Elijah and Elisha, about King Solomon and King David. At the end of 1 Samuel, when I read that David's friend Jonathan had died, I was very upset. Although this was an ancient book, I could feel the reality of the friendship between David and Jonathan. Bible stories just leapt out the page, connected with me, and inspired my imagination. The Bible was able to talk to me as a kid and make me interested in it. I knew it was true, but it proved difficult reconciling the peace of Yeshua with a stressful childhood in which I was always ill and unhappy both at home and at school.

Young Manhood

My school years were plagued with illness, and throughout my teenage years, as a believer in Yeshua, my fundamental assumption was that what I saw as Christianity was repressing me. I was told more about what I shouldn't and couldn't do than what I should and could! I wanted God to bless me or allow me to have something which I could show off. I wanted a nice, comfortable, healthy life like my mates, but for some reason God hadn't given me that, even though I was a believer! I began to read more and more of the Bible and saw how I should live and what I should do.

At school, in order to be consistent and to prevent people from calling me a hypocrite, I pretended to be holier than everyone else, so that they'd all see how good I was. But I wasn't good; so I had to pretend to be good in order to try to attract people to what I believed. For better or worse, this meant that many of my friends missed out on knowing the real me! I didn't realise that God was not calling me to be something I wasn't. When I was sixteen, things changed as I started going to a church that many teenagers attended. However, everyone there made light of the Bible; it was more of a social club, and people had no desire to really seek God. At seventeen, I went to a *Soul in the City* event in London, and that's when everything began to make sense.

Worth Nothing, but Delighted!

Soul in the City was an event where – primarily Gentile – teenagers who professed to be disciples of Jesus would reach out and provide social aid within the poorer areas of London. There was praise and teaching in the mornings, when all the teenagers gathered in one venue in East London. Every morning during the week, an American delivered a sermon to hundreds of young people. On the first day he spoke about how great God was, and how he had chosen Moses, not in spite of the fact that he was humble and insignificant, but because of it. I used to think that the heroes of the Tanakh were men who had done lots of good things in order to impress God, but here I was, discovering that God had chosen Moses before he'd done anything good. On the second day the speaker said that we were worth nothing! Most people might be a bit annoyed to hear that, but I was delighted. If we were all worthless before God, why should I feel so undermined all the time? Why did I need to feel that everyone else was somehow better than me? If none of us had any worth, what was the point of anything? Over the next few days, the speaker went on to explain how we could be used in God's plan. He told us that what mattered was not what God could do for us but what we would do for him!

Never a Doubt

The misfortune of growing up with parents who believe Yeshua is the Messiah is that it was totally natural to hear that Yeshua died for our sins. There was never a moment when I doubted it, but, perhaps, there was never a moment when I fully understood it either. I had treated Yeshua's death as something that didn't really matter. It was a case of familiarity breeding apathy. I felt that God had disappointed me simply because he hadn't given me what I wanted all the time. But suddenly my expectations and understanding of God had changed, and I knew he would not disappoint me. He had died in place of me, this I knew, but I realised something new – God didn't call me just to repent and believe but to repent, believe and *serve* him! I read the book of Ecclesiastes, written by King Solomon, and decided that the only thing that mattered was to serve God. It was so comforting to realise how pointless everything was, so why bother, unless your life is given meaning by God?

Searching for God

Everything came to a head at a youth conference I attended. I felt I was being introduced to something that looked to me like a mix of nightclub hedonism and Eastern mysticism. As I looked back on the experience a few days later, even though I had been sceptical at the time, I was disgusted by how I had allowed myself to be deceived. I spoke to my parents and others, read some books, and found there was a more biblical foundation on which I could base my life as a Jewish disciple of Yeshua.

I began to attend a Messianic Jewish Fellowship in East London, where I led the worship on the mandolin. This was great, but my parents went there too, and I felt I needed to find God by myself, and really discover the truth. I read Job, Proverbs and Ecclesiastes as often as I could in order to find the wisdom and insight to form a healthy worldview. A Bible study on Genesis 1-11 and Ecclesiastes with two close friends finally allowed me to really ask questions about who God was, and afterwards to feel that I'd actually learnt something.

Shalom at University

I was offered a place at the University of Leeds to read Spanish. I decided to accept the place and, in Leeds, I met a friend of the family. He could have been anyone – and I received the traditional, *You-don't-remember-me-do-you-because-when-I-last-saw-you-you-were-knee-high-to-a-grasshopper* greeting I always seemed to get from people who knew my parents: However, I went to his house, where I met his family and had an honest chat with him and his friend. These guys claimed to be disciples of the Jewish Messiah, and they were friends with many Jewish people who followed Yeshua. So I was still Jewish, and it wasn't just my parents who believed that this controversial combination could and should exist! When I went back to my halls, I felt very peaceful, as yet another piece of the jigsaw had fitted into place.

After I found Yeshua, I was able to give my brother some advice. He had become disillusioned with a church that was anti-Semitic and didn't take the Bible seriously. I had been messed about by churches that couldn't explain what they believed, and my parents had been forced out of their church by an anti-Semitic minister. The members of our family all have valid criticisms of how British churches treat Messianic Jews, which disillusioned us and separated us from true fellowship. It was refreshing for me therefore to meet other people who weren't afraid to challenge wrong attitudes in the church.

For the first time in my life, I joined a good church with sensible people! I was able to find out more about my Jewishness and to express it at a local Messianic Fellowship. I've never felt at home in churchy settings such as cell groups, as my bluntness and love of an honest debate often set me at odds with the nice people who just want to move on to the next bullet point. I've found the help and support of the Messianic Fellowship invaluable as I've challenged the university Christian Union to value the Jews, and I now have irrefutable evidence for God.

If anyone asks me if God exists, I tell them that I don't believe in a vague "god," I believe in the God of Israel. God chose the Jewish people, and despite centuries of persecution, the Jews still exist. The Crusades, the Inquisition, the Holocaust and the Arab nations could not *de-Jew* the Jew. The State of Israel is the size of Wales, yet it has outlasted mighty empires. The Egyptians fell; the Jews remained. The Babylonians fell; the Jews remained. The Greeks fell; the Jews remained. The great Romans fell; the Jews remained. The Third Reich fell; the Jews remained. What do you think will happen to Israel's current enemies?

God said in Isaiah 49 that he, the God of Israel, would be revealed to the world and, lo and behold, people from all nations and people groups now worship him and his son, the Jewish Rabbi, Yeshua the Messiah. The state of Israel is proof that God is the God of Israel and, as a Messianic Jew, I'm living proof that God hasn't finished with the Jewish people!

Now, with the Messiah of Israel in my heart, my Jewishness has flourished and I'm proud to call myself a *Messianic* Jew.

Shalom at the Jesus Tent!

Gerry

Back in 1971, while studying for my Bar Mitzvah ceremony, I was learning to translate Genesis 22, in which Abraham is told by God to take his dearly loved son Isaac to a mountain in order to sacrifice him. Well, you can imagine, I wasn't too impressed with God about that one. "I mean", I thought to myself, "I'll bet he wouldn't do it if *he* had a son!" I really thought I knew what God was all about until the July after my twelfth birthday.

The Finchley Carnival was a funfair held annually a couple of miles from my home. As I walked through the turnstile, I was handed a small piece of paper. It was an invitation to "Come to the Jesus Tent".

Shalom!
"Ha! I'll show them a thing or two," I thought to myself! I walked along, and the first marquee was the Baby Show

tent. I wasn't interested in that, but outside the next tent was a multi-lingual placard with words like: "Bienvenu", "Buenos Dias","Welcome" and "*Shalom*".

Talk about a red rag to a bull, or a bacon sandwich to a rabbi! "The Jesus Tent", eh? What right do these Christians have to use my Jewish language? Since when do Christians use the Jewish word Shalom? Oh boy! Am I gonna tell them a thing or two!

So in I went, a little five-foot zealot, like Paul on the road to Damascus,"breathing threats and murder against the church", as I would later read in Acts 9:1.

The Way, the Truth and the Life

I went in and was met by a very pleasant guy named Paul. I told him that I was concerned about the Christians using "my language".We talked for a long time, and he seemed genuinely interested in the fact that I was Jewish. We spoke about sin, forgiveness and all kinds of "religious" things like that. Paul showed me many of the promises that God had made about sending his Servant, the Messiah, things that were written in the Hebrew Bible – which most people call the Old Testament. I was absolutely amazed but didn't know what to do next. It was getting late and I had to cycle home, so I took a number of leaflets with me and thanked Paul for his time. That night I remembered something that was written on someone's tee shirt in the Tent: *Jesus said, "I am the Way, the Truth, and the Life. No-one comes to the Father except through Me".* (John 14:6)

Well, that was a really serious claim. I read about the way Jesus was put on trial, as prophesied over 700 years previously in Isaiah 53; how he was condemned to death and suffered the terrible agony of crucifixion

– prophesied centuries earlier in Psalm 22; and how finally, after dying and having a spear thrust into his side, he was buried. Perhaps not "finally" after all. I then read about his resurrection from the dead, also prophesied in Isaiah 53. I then came back to one other verse, John 3:16: "God loved the world so much that He gave His one and only Son, so that anyone who believes in Him will not die but will live for ever."

Now what was it I had thought about Abraham? How unfair it was of God to tell Abraham to put the wood on his son's back, to take him up the hill, to offer him as a sacrifice? And yet here was Jesus, *God's* beloved Son, with the wood of the crossbeam on his back, going up the hill to the place of crucifixion, to be offered as a sacrifice, once for all time.

The following night, I went back to the carnival.

Talking to God, Knowing God

As I approached the Jesus Tent, I started to cry. I found myself weeping because in a small way I'd begun to see the life I'd lived. I used to steal, to lie, to cheat; I used to be so deceitful; I was argumentative, I was very selfish. I wasn't worthy to stand before God.

I went into the tent and sat down at a table. Someone was singing an old song,

> Put your hand in the hand of the Man who stilled the waters,
> Put your hand in the hand of the Man who calmed the sea.

I really wanted peace. In the midst of the storms of life, I wanted peace.

Someone came up to me, sat down and put his arm round my shoulder. "Is there anything we can do?" he asked.

I just blurted out how I felt – that, in the words of the Bible, I was a sinner. I was no good in God's sight. The young man simply said that he knew God loved me so very much, and that Jesus really did die to take away my guilt and everything that stood in the way of me having a real relationship with God as my Father. By this time, a few others had gathered round as we talked. Finally the young man asked me, "Do you want to know Jesus?"

My response was immediate: "Yes, I do." So he prayed a simple prayer, talking naturally to God, his heavenly Father. Amazingly, he started by thanking God for creating me, thanking him for loving me, for bringing me to the tent and thanking Jesus for dying and rising for me.

Then he asked me if I would say a prayer with him. I repeated some simple phrases after him, talking to God in a real way for the first time in my life. I said how sorry I was for my past. I thanked Yeshua for giving me the chance of a brand new life. And then I asked Yeshua to come and live within me by his power.

Suddenly, it was as if fireworks had gone off inside me! My whole body – inside and out – felt washed by a powerful burst of energy like a strong waterfall. My eyes became sharp, my hearing became clear, everything became vibrant and real, and I knew, I *knew* that I had been forgiven. Now I was laughing and crying with tears of joy and happiness! I knew beyond doubt that everything written about Jesus was true. It was real! Yeshua was alive!

I knew from that moment on, even though I would fail him and would stumble my way into heaven, that Yeshua would be with me for all time, and for eternity as my Best Friend, Guide, Shepherd, God and King!!

Within a short while, I was outside the tent telling people about what had just happened. I began to go to church, and although I often let my Messiah down, I knew then, as I know now, that my life would never be the same. Yeshua has made all the difference. Thank God!

What Has Remained!

A year or two ago I went up to London and drove past the place where, nearly thirty years ago, I first really heard that amazing news about Jesus – Yeshua – the Messiah. I then went a couple of miles down the road and stood outside the house where my family had lived for so long. It was raining. The conifer trees still smelled the way they used to the day my father laid the tarmac in the drive. I remembered him building the garage.

I remembered cutting the hedge, washing the car, mowing the grass. And now? Now other people live there. Other people cut the grass; other people drive their cars in and out, use the front door and sit in the garden. What has happened since the day I left that house?

My life has changed so very much. The days and months, years and seasons have turned around. I have grown up, worked, married, separated, divorced, studied, been well-off, been poor, learned to drive, dated women, been single, gained weight, slimmed down, gained weight again (it's all the latkes!). I've even grown a beard. I've been leading worship and preaching for nearly thirty years, and I've been leading a Messianic Fellowship for over five years. Now I am married to a wonderful woman who is caring, supportive, spiritual and special. I graduated from University in 2004 with an honours degree, and I have since finished post-graduate training to be a Secondary School RE teacher. But what has remained? What has been constant in all this? Simply this; that Yeshua my Messiah has never forgotten me, nor has he ever forsaken me.

Glossary

Items marked * have a separate entry.

Afikomen. A Greek word believed by some scholars to mean, "He is coming". At the Passover Seder*, three pieces of matzah*, or unleavened bread are kept in a cloth bag called a matzah tash. During the Seder the middle matzah, or Afikomen, is removed, broken and hidden away until the end of the evening.

Aliyah. Hebrew for "going up". Jewish people "make aliyah" when they immigrate to Israel to become permanent citizens.

Bar Mitzvah. "Son of the Commandment". At the age of thirteen, Jewish boys come of age. They are called up to read the Torah* portion and Haftorah* in the synagogue.

Bat Chayil/Bat Mitzvah. "Daughter of Worth". A coming-of-age ceremony for a Jewish girl.

Brit (Bris) Mila. Circumcision.

Bris certificate. A *bris* certificate is presented to the parents of Jewish boys after their circumcision.

Cheder/Heder. Hebrew for "room". A supplementary school attached to a synagogue at which Jewish children learn about their culture and religion, usually on Sundays.

Erev Shabbat. Hebrew: "Sabbath Eve", Friday evening at sunset when Shabbat starts.

Farshmak. Traditional Jewish fish dish.

Frum. Someone who is an observant Orthodox Jew.

Gefiltefish. Traditional Jewish fish dish.

Gemarah. A commentary on the Hebrew Scriptures

Goyim. Hebrew for "nations". A term for Gentiles or non-Jews.

Haftorah. The weekly reading from the Prophets and Writings in the Tanakh* to accompany and complement the Torah* reading.

Haggadah. The Passover order of service.

Hanukkah. The Feast of Dedication that celebrates the rededication of the Temple in Jerusalem after the Maccabees liberated it from the Syrian king Antiochus Epiphanes.

Haredim. The preferred self-definition of ultra-orthodox Jews. The literal meaning comes from the Hebrew word to fear, thus a Hared is one who is in awe of God.

Kabbalat Shabbat. Literally, "receiving the Sabbath". The Friday evening celebration of the start of the Sabbath.

Kaddish. The Aramaic word for "holy". The ancient Jewish "mourners' prayer".

Kapparah. The Hebrew word for atonement.

Kiddush. Home-based Shabbat ceremony to thank God for the fruit of the vine and the fruit of the earth.

Kneidalach. Matzah*-based dumplings.

Kosher. From the Hebrew word for "fit". According to Jewish law, only food that is "fit" may be consumed. Although the Bible prescribes which foods are permissible for Jews, an elaborate set of laws and rituals have been added to the biblical regulations, including the prohibition on eating meat and dairy products together.

Latkes. Potato pancakes, traditionally eaten at the festival of Hanukkah*.

Maftir: The final section of the weekly Torah* portion read in Synagogue on Shabbat*.

Mashiach. The Hebrew word for Messiah which when translated into Greek is Christos.

Matzah. Unleavened bread eaten especially at Passover*.

Meshuggeh. Yiddish for crazy, a nutter.

Mezuzah. A ceremonial box nailed to the doors of Jewish homes with a Bible passage on a scroll inside.

Mezuzot. Plural of Mezuzah.*

Minyan. Hebrew: "Number". Public services cannot take place in a synagogue unless a minimum of ten Jewish men are present. A Minyan is the minimum number of men required.

Moshiach. The Yiddish* pronunciation of the word Mashiach.*

Pesach. Passover, the festival at which the Jewish people remember and celebrate the redemption of the children of Israel from Egypt.

Purim. The Festival of Lots, recorded in the book of Esther, which celebrates the deliverance of the Jewish people from the genocidal conspiracy of Haman.

Rosh HaShanah. Jewish New Year.

Seder. The meal eaten at Passover*, following an order of service called a Haggadah*.

Shabbat. The Jewish "Sabbath" begins at sunset on Friday and concludes at sunset on Saturday.

Shavuot. Pentecost. The Feast of Weeks.

Sheeney. A vulgar term of contempt, possibly derived from the Russian word *zhid* or the Polish word *zid*.

Shema: Hebrew prayer from Deuteronomy 6:4-9.

Shul. Synagogue.

Simchat Torah. "Rejoicing the Law", a celebration of the completion of the annual cycle of Torah* and Haftorah* Synagogue readings.

Succot: Feast of Tabernacles.

Talmud. A massive collection of writings, recording the discussions of the great Jewish sages. According to the Jewish scholar Jacob Neusner and others, the Talmud is the supreme authority in Judaism.

Tanakh. A Hebrew acronym for the Old Testament, which is divided into three sections: **T**orah*, **N**eviim, **K**etuvim – The Law, the Prophets and the Writings.

Torah. The Five Books of Moses: or **Torah**. The Five books of Moses: Genesis, Exodus, Leviticus, Numbers and Deuteronomy.

Tsimess. Chicken and carrot stew.

Yeshua. The Hebrew form of the name Jesus.

Yiddish. European Jewish language, mix of Hebrew and German.

Yom Kippur. The Day of Atonement.

**Other books of interest from
Christian Focus Publications**

The
Importance
of being
Ernest

A Jewish Life spent in Christian Mission

'an inspiration to me...
a great read'
Helen Shapiro

Mike Moore

The Importance of Being Ernest
A Jewish Life spent in Christian Mission
Mike Moore

Ernest Lloyd's life spans almost the entire twentieth century. At the age of six he was placed in the care of the Naomi Children's Home run by the Barbican Mission to the Jews and in his teens he came to faith in Jesus as his Messiah.

At the age of twenty he became a missionary with the British Jews Society and for seventy years he has travelled the globe as a missionary to his own people and as an ambassador of Jewish mission. He has also played a major role in the birth and growth of the modern Messianic Jewish movement. The book chronicles the important role Ernest played in Jewish mission during the twentieth century and how, through his ministry, many Jews and Gentiles, including entire families, have come to know the Messiah. The book also provides insights into Jewish life, culture and religion.

ISBN 978 1 85792 806 8

YOU'LL GO TO LONDON
THE AUTOBIOGRAPHY OF LIONEL BALL

You'll Go to London
The Autobiography of Lionel Ball
Lionel Ball

Lionel Ball served as a London City Missionary most of his working life. A whole generation of London City Missionaries are grateful to God for the encouragement given to them by him. Even today, some years after his retirement, missionaries regularly meet people who ask, 'Do you remember Lionel Ball?'

Through his chaplaincy with the police, he was so highly regarded that he was appointed a Freeman of the City of London. This meant that he could drive sheep across London Bridge without paying. There is no record of him ever taking advantage of the privilege. Instead Lionel was to undertake a different sort of shepherding!

The key place he worked was at the Covent Garden Mission but Lionel was also involved in mission activity in the London theatres. Blessed with a fine voice, and himself a gifted pianist, he related well to performers and won their confidence and love. There are many who can trace their early Christian influence back to Lionel Ball.

Lionel Ball has spents years gaining the respect of Londoners through his work with the London City Mission. Through his chaplaincy with the police he was granted freedom of the city.

ISBN 978 1 84550 314 7

Tell Me The Story
The Carpenter
Alex MacDonald

Alex retells these eye-witness stories of Jesus. These people tell their stories as eye witnesses of those who were actually there. They are:

Mary, mother of Jesus, Gaius Maximus, centurion, Joanna's story of John The Baptist, woman at the well, Simon the Pharisee, Gadarene Demoniac, Jairus, Simon Peter, Rich ruler, Bartimaeus & Zacchaeus, John and Marcellus a Roman officer.

Using Biblical, contemporary and background data, Alex MacDonald skilfully tells the stories of those who were with Jesus at key points in his life.

It unfolds as if you were on the spot looking on. The stories are based on factual evidence of what really happened. This book will capture your imagination causing you to ask "What would my reaction have been if I had been there?" or "Was this really what happened"?

Alex MacDonald is the minister of Buccleuch & Greyfriars Free Church of Scotland, Edinburgh. He is married to Evelyn and they have four Children, Katharine, Douglas, Alison and Robert.

ISBN 978 1 84550 285 0